The Complete Cuisinart Air Fryer Oven Cookbook for Beginners

1000 Everyday Recipes To Take Care Of Friends And Family With The Ultimate And Time-Saving Guide To Cook Delightful And Easy Meals.

SOPHIA SANDERSON

what do you find inside?

Sophia
SANDERSON

Sophia Sanderson 58 years old, she attended one of the best courses at La Cuisine de Marie-Blanche-France, in Paris, coming out with top marks.

Writer, cook and activist Sophia Sanderson is the author of several cookbooks.

She is an expert in many and different diets, she wanted to write them on paper by inventing, re-studying and taking inspiration from the wonderful recipes, her books are therefore the result of 8 years of work.

She is now the head cook in her successful restaurants, and with the help of her chef collaborators she brings tradition and innovation into their kitchens, and it is often the place where her recipes are born!

Harmony, precision and determination distinguish Sophia and her recipes.

TABLE OF CONTENTS

Chapter 5 Snack & Appetizer   70

Chapter 6 Fish & Seafood 86

Chapter 7 Vegetables 97

Introduction

This Air fryer Oven Cookbook contains easy, delicious, and healthy recipes that can be prepared within few minutes. It is highly recommended for people with busy schedules and also for those on the Weight Watchers Program.

Even if you have never tried the Air Fryer Oven before, it promises you one thing, after having this cookbook, you will be kicking yourself for having not discovered this sooner.

It will inspire you to clean up your kitchen from all the useless appliances that clutter your countertop and start putting the Air Fryer Oven to good use. The air fryer oven will give you lots of joy, time, and, most importantly, tasty dishes. Feel free to adjust and alter these recipes, or simply use them as a springboard of inspiration for your own creations!

The Air Fryer Oven is definitely a change in lifestyle that will make things much easier for you and your family. You'll discover increased energy, decreased hunger, a boosted metabolism, and of course, a LOT of free time! You will know that it is not just a simple kitchen appliance. Still, it's truly a kitchen-miracle that will bring relief and satisfaction with its user-friendly functions, time plus energy-effective heating method, and multiple cooking options. This cookbook will share as many different recipes to provide an extensive guideline to all the frequent oven users. With the latest air fryer oven functions, you can air fry, dehydrate, broil, toast, roast, and bake all kinds of the dishes. Please give it a full read and find out tons of new ways to add more colors and flavors to your dinner table using the Air fryer Oven.

Why Use an Air Fryer Oven?

First and foremost, the air fryer oven became popular for its numerous health benefits. The convenience and ease of using an air fryer oven give an effortless choice for people that wants a healthy and delicious meal in a matter of time. For those who are hesitant on the air fryer oven potential and favor the conventional cooking way, perhaps the following benefits are enough to assure them to make the switch to efficient cooking:

Great for cooking solidified foods without oil and extraordinary or pre-heating foods.

Because of littler bins, the food cooked speedier when contrasted with ovens, and no pre-heating is fundamental.

The kind of food is brilliant because the heat gives a pleasantly fresh and does not burn.

Perfect for two individuals or littler segments. There's such a significant number of greater models out there to cook bigger parts for multiple individuals. The potential outcomes are inestimable.

It's a healthier method of cooking fried or crispy foods. In general, you can utilize substantially less oil to accomplish crunchy and crispy finished foods.

There's tidy little up and less splattering of oil while cooking. Everything gets contained pleasantly inside the air fryer while cooking.

Food cooks fresh due to the littler cooking zone, and the heating component is nearer to the food.

There's no need to warm up your home in summer when you're longing for something warm, roasted, or pan-fried.

What features does an air fryer toaster oven have that a convection oven does not?

Air fryers and convection ovens have a bunch of similarities. The previously mentioned sight-seeing circulation is among the most significant attributes when looking at these gadgets. We'll attempt to look past those similitudes when contrasting them. Subsequently, you'll get a separation of the main highlights of both convection ovens and air fryers. Along these lines, you'll have the option to figure out which one is all the more engaging for your situation.

In contrast to normal traditional ovens, the best convection ovens, for example, breville bov800xl, convey the sight-seeing evenly. Convection ovens, for example, modify the temperature naturally once you place the food in them. This element allows you to try different things with an assortment of dishes.

Convection ovens are typically huge and appropriate for large courses. They offer enough space for a scope of various culinary encounters. With convection ovens, you don't need to stress over your food winding up undercooked. The air dissemination arrives at the center of the food, much the same as it forms the edges.

There are a number of air fryer brands, among which we essentially should specify phillips air fryer, represent a culinary development. While cooking with a convection oven you will end up using a larger portion of oil, but with an air fryer toaster oven it wouldn't be necessary. Most air fryers have a container where you place the food you need to cook. Despite the fact that they arrive at the pinnacle of their exhibition in singing, you can attempt different strategies with a significant number of them.

The most significant component of air fryers, for example, power xl air fryer, is that you can put them on your

kitchen counter. They are sufficiently minimized to remain on the counter without occupying an excess of room. In the clash of convection ovens versus air fryers, it's essential to call attention to the temperature. As a rule, air fryers arrive at higher temperatures, and are in this way, progressively helpful for sensitive suppers, for example, treats. Convection ovens will, in general, be somewhat excessively hard on this sort of dish.

When examining air fryers versus convection ovens, we could state that air fryers are increasingly helpful on account of the ledge arrangement. In any case, remember that there are convection ovens, for example, convection toaster oven, which is a ledge, also.

Is using an air fryer toaster oven healthier than cooking in a convection oven?

The path both of these gadgets treat the food is amazingly healthy. Convection ovens and air fryers take part in a comparative strategy, which includes sight-seeing circulation. Most of the two classes use fans which deliver and empower the tourist flow all through the unit.

It's critical to bring up the way that, in contrast to regular ovens, these gadgets don't have heating components. The presence of heating components confines the temperature to the zone, which is the closest.

Since this is a relative convection oven versus air fryer survey, we should see which one leads the pack with regards to healthiness.

Enter your convection ovens do offer various conceivable outcomes. You can cook anything you might envision in these ovens. In contrast to broiling skillet or profound fryers, you can include a modest quantity of oil to your dish. The food will cook in its regular juices, with no compelling reason to include abundance oil. Thusly you can get the characteristic sauce in case you're handling meat.

Then again, the healthier decision on account of convection ovens versus air fryers could be the air fryers.

Upon al, a large portion of the air fryers requires no expansion of oil by any stretch of the imagination. The prefix oil-less stands nearby many air fryers. When preparing or searing in a convection oven, you'll likely add some oil to include some dampness.

Air fryers arrive at higher temperatures. Along these lines, the cooking procedure with them is shorter. Along these lines, your food doesn't dry, and it finds a workable pace healthy fixings. If you utilize the oven to slow-cook, a lot of supplements can evaporate simultaneously.

In any case, cooking with less to no oil is an incredible option for some cooking systems out there.

In terms of size and cooking capacity, would a convection oven be better than an air fryer toaster?

These two factors enormously impact the decision of any purchaser, paying little heed to some other components. The quantity of the unit matters since you should adjust it to your kitchen space. There's nothing more awful than having kitchen supplies, which limit your development in the kitchen. This sort of pickle can likewise be hazardous, and it can cause breaking and harming.

To the extent the cooking limit goes, this is a totally abstract issue. You know about your cooking capacities and requirements. Regarding those elements, pick the comparing cooking limit.

Presently, how about we see what to convection ovens and air fryers bring to the table in these particular angles. Convection ovens are generally greater than air fryers.

Their arrangement is normally not ledge, so a few people discover them not as agreeable as the air fryers. Likewise, you need to curve to put the food into it, to screen the cooking procedure, lastly, to take the food out. This sort of situating might be awkward for you. Air fryers are littler and increasingly smaller in size. In this manner, they can be placed snugly on your kitchen counters, making for ease of access and use. Air fryers are simpler to clean and store, which we will talk about later.

The greater the size – the greater the cooking limit. For the most part, you'll see that this standard applies to kitchen supplies. Justifiably, air fryers and convection ovens are the same. Since convection ovens are greater, their cooking limit is typically bigger. This implies it'll allow you to cook more food without a moment's delay. Also, you'll have the option to put greater pieces of food in it without slashing it.

Then again, because of their shape, air fryers, for the most part, have a littler cooking limit. Don't let this dolt you. Many air fryers have profound chambers in which you can put a lot of food, for example, french fries. In any case, you won't have the option to roast sheep legs or greater pieces like such.

Is an air fryer toaster oven easier to maintain than a convection oven?

No one needs to go through an excess of cash or cash, keeping up their culinary gadgets. Food dribbling, oil splatter, and steady stains can cause a wreck in your kitchen. In case you're not an enthusiast of cleaning, you'll welcome an air fryer much in excess of a convection oven.

Some air fryers come equipped with a non-stick container, which will take you just several minutes to clean off. Their inside, just as outside, contains material that doesn't raise any

ruckus during cleaning. Likewise, air fryers are littler, and you'll certainly invest less energy looking after it. Its versatility is likewise useful.

With regards to support, convection ovens do will, in general reason some cerebral pain. Convection oven proprietors should focus on and truly get in there. Their situation additionally makes it difficult to arrive at each and every region of the unit. The developed stains and trickling can be very difficult to dispose of. If there should be an occurrence of convection oven cleaning, you'll most likely need to utilize solid cleansers so as to leave it totally perfect.

Reliability is a relative subject that is difficult to characterize. In this way, it is mistaken to state that both of these classes gives greater unwavering quality. What decides are the materials, the nature of the unit, the settings, and a couple of different parts.

Along these lines, to make certain of dependability, you should respect it for every gadget independently. Give close a to the nature of the structure and the life span of the material. Likewise, the guarantee assumes a noteworthy job in this perspective. A decent guarantee will give you a feeling that all is well with the world, paying little mind to different variables.

On the off chance that we were to by and large talk about unwavering quality, maybe the normally treated steel plan of convection ovens is

Increasingly alluring.

It is difficult to decide the victor of this convection oven versus air fryer fight. As should be obvious, there are numerous likenesses, and you can draw an equal between these two classes. Likewise, we focused on a portion of the unmistakable highlights of every one of the gadgets.

You can settle on your choice by picking the gadget which contains the most noteworthy number of your preferred qualities.

Despite your choice, it's essential to call attention to that you can't turn out badly with both of these. Consider your desires and your potential outcomes, and "flip the coin."

You can adapt your favorite stove-top dish so it becomes air fryer toaster oven–friendly. It all boils down to variety and lots of options.

Cooking perfect and delicious as well as healthy meals has never been easier.

Remember to clean your air fryer oven and accessories according to the instructions and safety precautions after each cooking adventure. Like every appliance, maintenance is needed to get what you would like in the device. Any tool employed for preparing food must be stored spotlessly clean. Don't let dirt develop and clean the environment fryer frequently, so you get great results when you make use of the air fryer oven. You have to make sure you remember it, "keep clean and maintain it" for best results efficiently because taken care of the appliance will always last longer. We provide you with some cleaning tips; however, it is not difficult. The outdoors and inside parts could be cleaned relatively easily and ought to be done frequently. Within the situation from the heating coil, get it done a couple of occasions annually only.

With so many recipes and a comprehensive guideline about the air fryer oven, you will know how to put to its best use and enjoy a range of flavorsome crispy meals in no time. This ten in one multipurpose kitchen miracle has brought much-wanted peace and comfort to the homemakers' lives who can now cook a healthy and delicious meal for their family in no time. This cookbook's different segment provides a step-by-step direction to cook various meals ranging from breakfast, poultry, meat, vegetables, snacks, and much more. Get this latest hit Air Fryer Oven Cookbook and bring convenience to your kitchen floor now. If you had an air fryer oven and you don't know what to cook in it, now you do – with all the recipes at its best!

What are you still waiting for? Start cooking in your air fryer oven and enjoy all the foods you thought were not healthy!

Chapter 1. How to Use Breville Smart Air Fryer Oven? `

The Fryer Oven features advanced digital controls that allow you maximum flexibility and accuracy. Still, it also harnesses the power of convection cooking for faster and evener cooking. And because it features an ample cooking space, you can prepare a wide variety of different dishes without using your regular oven.

What Does It Not Do?

The Air Fryer is a marvel of functionality. From convection cooking to perfect defrosting, it does so many things. But there are a few things it can't do.

This kind of air fryer oven will not take your microwave place because it will not heat food as quickly. It does, however, heat up much faster than a conventional oven. You are also somewhat limited by the size of it.

While it does feature a large cooking compartment, you will not be able to cook a twenty-pound turkey in it. Other than these few limitations, Air Fryer Oven can handle most of your cooking needs.

Who Is It Not Good For?

While this is perfect for nearly any situation, if you have limited space in your kitchen and do not need another cooking appliance, this oven may not be for you. Also, if your family prefers only to make large meals, the small size of this Air Fryer Oven may not be large enough to meet your needs.

How to Use Air Fryer Oven?

Your air fryer oven really couldn't be easier to use. The following are some steps to help you get going!

Step 1: Start by checking all the components and see if they are in good shape, especially the power cord, because any fault in the power cord can be hazardous.

Step 2: Remove the air fryer oven from the box, then place it on a level surface near a grounded power outlet. Plug the air fryer oven.

Step 3: Remove the trays from the air fryer oven. (Before using the air fryer oven, make sure to clean the trays with soap and water thoroughly.) Right after unboxing the device, it is essential to clean the appliance inside out using a clean piece of cloth and wash all the oven's removable accessories before the use.

Step4: Set the oven to the Pizza function and use the Time button to select 18 minutes.

Step 5: Press the Start button and allow finishing the cooking cycle. Once the cooking cycle has finished, your Oven is ready to use.

Learning the Controls

The great thing about Air Fryer Oven is that all the controls are labeled for easy use, so you don't have to bother with confusing dials.

Function Knob:

This knob allows you to select which cooking program you would like. Choose from Toast, Bake, Broil, Roast, Cookies, Reheat, Pizza, and Bagel.

LCD Display:

Displays the number of pieces of bread, darkness setting; Current time; Cooking temperature, and amount of time left to cook.

Temp/Darkness Button:

Select the temperature or darkness setting for the toast.

Up and Down Selection Buttons:

Use to adjust time, temperature, and amount of darkness.

Time/Slices Button:

Use to adjust the cooking time and number of slices of bread.

A Bit More:

This function adds a small amount of cooking time. The amount of time varies depending on which cooking program you have chosen.

Start/Cancel Button:

It starts and stops the cooking process.

F/C Button:

Choose Fahrenheit or Celsius.

Frozen Foods Button:

Adds extra time to the cooking process to defrost frozen foods.

Chapter 2 Breakfast Recipes

Protein Banana Bread

Prep Time	Cook Time	Serving
10 Minutes	1 hour 10 Minutes	16

Ingredients

- 3 eggs
- 1/3 cup coconut flour
- 1/2 cup Swerve
- 2 cups almond flour
- 1/2 cup ground chia seed
- 1/2 tsp vanilla extract
- 4 tbsp butter, melted
- 3/4 cup almond milk
- 1 tbsp baking powder
- 1/3 cup protein powder
- 1/2 cup water
- 1/2 tsp salt

Directions

1. Grease loaf pan with butter and set aside.
2. Insert wire rack in rack position 6. Select bake, set temperature 325 F, timer for 1 hour 10 minutes. Press start to preheat the oven.
3. In a small bowl, whisk together chia seed and 1/2 cup water. Set aside.
4. In a large bowl, mix together almond flour, baking powder, protein powder, coconut flour, sweetener, and salt.
5. Stir in eggs, milk, chia seed mixture, vanilla extract, and butter until well combined.
6. Pour batter into the prepared loaf pan and bake for 1 hour 10 minutes.
7. Sliced and serve.

Nutritional Value (Amount per Serving):
- Calories 162
- Fat 13.4 g
- Carbohydrates 6 g
- Sugar 0.5 g
- Protein 5.2 g
- Cholesterol 40 mg

Cheese Soufflés

Prep Time	Cook Time	Serving
10 Minutes	25 Minutes	8

Ingredients

- 6 eggs, separated
- 3/4 cup heavy cream
- 1/4 tsp cayenne pepper
- 1/2 tsp xanthan gum
- 1/2 tsp pepper
- 1/4 tsp cream of tartar
- 1/4 cup chives, chopped
- 2 cups cheddar cheese, shredded
- 1 tsp ground mustard
- 1 tsp salt

Directions

1. Spray 8 ramekins with cooking spray and place on a baking sheet.
2. Insert wire rack in rack position 6. Select bake, set temperature 350 F, timer for 25 minutes. Press start to preheat the oven.
3. In a large bowl, mix together almond flour, cayenne pepper, pepper, mustard, salt, and xanthan gum.
4. Add heavy cream and stir to combine.
5. Whisk in egg yolks, chives, and cheese until combined.
6. In a mixing bowl, add egg whites and cream of tartar and beat until stiff peaks form.
7. Fold egg white mixture into the almond flour mixture until combined.
8. Pour mixture into the ramekins and bake for 25 minutes.
9. Serve and enjoy.

Nutritional Value (Amount per Serving):
- Calories 204
- Fat 16.9 g
- Carbohydrates 2.3 g
- Sugar 0.5 g
- Protein 11.7 g
- Cholesterol 168 mg

Easy Kale Muffins

Prep Time	Cook Time	Serving
10 Minutes	30 Minutes	8

Ingredients

- 6 eggs
- 1/2 cup milk
- 1/4 cup chives, chopped
- 1 cup kale, chopped
- Pepper
- Salt

Directions

1. Spray 8 cups muffin pan with cooking spray and set aside.
2. Insert wire rack in rack position 6. Select bake, set temperature 350 F, timer for 30 minutes. Press start to preheat the oven.
3. Add all ingredients into the mixing bowl and whisk well.
4. Pour mixture into the prepared muffin pan and bake for 30 minutes.
5. Serve and enjoy.

Nutritional Value (Amount per Serving):
- Calories 59
- Fat 3.6 g
- Carbohydrates 2 g
- Sugar 1 g
- Protein 5 g
- Cholesterol 124 mg

Mozzarella Spinach Quiche

Prep Time	Cook Time	Serving
10 Minutes	45 Minutes	6

Ingredients

- 4 eggs
- 10 oz frozen spinach, thawed
- 1/2 cup mozzarella cheese, shredded
- 1/4 cup parmesan cheese, grated
- 8 oz mushrooms, sliced
- 2 oz feta cheese, crumbled
- 1 cup almond milk
- 1 garlic clove, minced
- Pepper
- Salt

Directions

1. Spray a pie dish with cooking spray and set aside.
2. Insert wire rack in rack position 6. Select bake, set temperature 350 F, timer for 45 minutes. Press start to preheat the oven.
3. Spray medium pan with cooking spray and heat over medium heat.
4. Add garlic, mushrooms, pepper, and salt in a pan and sauté for 5 minutes.
5. Add spinach in pie dish then add sautéed mushroom on top of spinach.
6. Sprinkle feta cheese over spinach and mushroom.
7. In a bowl, whisk eggs, parmesan cheese, and almond milk.
8. Pour egg mixture over spinach and mushroom then sprinkle shredded mozzarella cheese and bake for 45 minutes.
9. Sliced and serve.

Nutritional Value (Amount per Serving):
- Calories 197
- Fat 16 g
- Carbohydrates 6.2 g
- Sugar 2.8 g
- Protein 10.4 g
- Cholesterol 121 mg

Cheesy Zucchini Quiche

Prep Time	Cook Time	Serving
10 Minutes	60 Minutes	8

Ingredients

- 2 eggs
- 2 cups cheddar cheese, shredded
- 2 lbs zucchini, sliced
- 1 1/2 cup almond milk
- Pepper
- Salt

Directions

1. Grease quiche pan with cooking spray and set aside.
2. Insert wire rack in rack position 6. Select bake, set temperature 375 F, timer for 60 minutes. Press start to preheat the oven.
3. Season zucchini with pepper and salt and set aside for 30 minutes.
4. In a large bowl, whisk eggs with almond milk, pepper, and salt.
5. Add shredded cheddar cheese and stir well.
6. Arrange zucchini slices in quiche pan.
7. Pour egg mixture over zucchini slices then sprinkle with shredded cheese.
8. Bake for 60 minutes.
9. Serve and enjoy.

Nutritional Value (Amount per Serving):
- Calories 251
- Fat 21.4 g
- Carbohydrates 6.7 g
- Sugar 3.7 g
- Protein 10.8 g
- Cholesterol 71 mg

Healthy Asparagus Quiche

Prep Time	Cook Time	Serving
10 Minutes	60 Minutes	6

Ingredients

- 5 eggs, beaten
- 1 cup almond milk
- 15 asparagus spears, cut ends then cut asparagus in half
- 1 cup Swiss cheese, shredded
- 1/4 tsp thyme
- 1/4 tsp white pepper
- 1/4 tsp salt

Directions

1. Grease quiche pan with cooking spray and set aside.
2. Insert wire rack in rack position 6. Select bake, set temperature 350 F, timer for 60 minutes. Press start to preheat the oven.
3. In a bowl, whisk together eggs, thyme, white pepper, almond milk, and salt.
4. Arrange asparagus in quiche pan then pour egg mixture over asparagus. Sprinkle with shredded cheese.
5. Bake for 60 minutes.
6. Sliced and serve.

Nutritional Value (Amount per Serving):
- Calories 225
- Fat 18.3 g
- Carbohydrates 5.9 g
- Sugar 3 g
- Protein 11.7 g
- Cholesterol 153 mg

Mini Veggie Quiche Cups

Prep Time	Cook Time	Serving
10 Minutes	20 Minutes	12

Ingredients

- 8 eggs
- 3/4 cup cheddar cheese, shredded
- 10 oz frozen spinach, chopped
- 1/4 cup onion, chopped
- 1/4 cup mushroom, diced
- 1/4 cup bell pepper, diced

Directions

1. Spray 12 cups muffin pan with cooking spray and set aside.
2. Insert wire rack in rack position 6. Select bake, set temperature 375 F, timer for 20 minutes. Press start to preheat the oven.
3. Add all ingredients into the mixing bowl and beat until combine.
4. Pour egg mixture into the prepared muffin pan and bake for 20 minutes.
5. Serve and enjoy.

Nutritional Value (Amount per Serving):
- Calories 78
- Fat 5.4 g
- Carbohydrates 1.6 g
- Sugar 0.6 g
- Protein 6.2 g
- Cholesterol 117 mg

Lemon Blueberry Muffins

Prep Time	Cook Time	Serving
10 Minutes	25 Minutes	12

Ingredients

- 2 eggs
- 1 tsp baking powder
- 5 drops stevia
- 1/4 cup butter, melted
- 1 cup heavy whipping cream
- 2 cups almond flour
- 1/4 tsp lemon zest
- 1/2 tsp lemon extract
- 1/2 cup fresh blueberries

Directions

1. Spray 12 cups muffin pan with cooking spray and set aside.
2. Insert wire rack in rack position 6. Select bake, set temperature 350 F, timer for 25 minutes. Press start to preheat the oven.
3. In a mixing bowl, whisk eggs.
4. Add remaining ingredients to the eggs and mix until well combined.
5. Pour batter into the prepared muffin pan and bake for 25 minutes.
6. Serve and enjoy.

Nutritional Value (Amount per Serving):
- Calories 195
- Fat 17.2 g
- Carbohydrates 5.4 g
- Sugar 0.7 g
- Protein 5.2 g
- Cholesterol 51 mg

Baked Breakfast Donuts

Prep Time	Cook Time	Serving
10 Minutes	20 Minutes	6

Ingredients

- 4 eggs
- 1/3 cup almond milk
- 1 tbsp liquid stevia
- 3 tbsp cocoa powder
- 1/4 cup coconut oil
- 1/3 cup coconut flour
- 1/2 tsp baking soda
- 1/2 tsp baking powder
- 1/2 tsp instant coffee

Directions

1. Spray donut pan with cooking spray and set aside.
2. Insert wire rack in rack position 6. Select bake, set temperature 350 F, timer for 20 minutes. Press start to preheat the oven.
3. Add all ingredients into the mixing bowl and mix until well combined.
4. Pour batter into the donut pan and bake for 20 minutes.
5. Serve and enjoy.

Nutritional Value (Amount per Serving):
- Calories 184
- Fat 16.2 g
- Carbohydrates 7.1 g
- Sugar 0.7 g
- Protein 5.4 g
- Cholesterol 109 mg

Blueberry Almond Muffins

Prep Time	Cook Time	Serving
10 Minutes	15 Minutes	8

Ingredients

- 1 egg
- 3/4 cup heavy cream
- 1/4 cup butter
- 1/4 tsp baking powder
- 2 1/2 cup almond flour
- 1/2 cup fresh blueberries
- 1/2 tsp baking soda
- 5 drops liquid stevia
- 1/4 tsp vanilla extract
- 1/2 tsp salt

Directions

1. Spray 8 cups muffin pan with cooking spray and set aside.
2. Insert wire rack in rack position 6. Select bake, set temperature 375 F, timer for 15 minutes. Press start to preheat the oven.
3. In a bowl, mix together almond flour, salt, and baking powder.
4. In a large bowl, whisk together egg, butter, vanilla, stevia, baking soda, and heavy cream.
5. Add almond flour mixture into the egg mixture and stir to combine.
6. Pour batter into the muffin pan and bake for 15 minutes.
7. Serve and enjoy.

Nutritional Value (Amount per Serving):
- Calories 313
- Fat 27.1 g
- Carbohydrates 9.3 g
- Sugar 1 g
- Protein 8.6 g
- Cholesterol 51 mg

Feta Broccoli Frittata

Prep Time	Cook Time	Serving
10 Minutes	20 Minutes	4

Ingredients

- 10 eggs
- 2 oz feta cheese, crumbled
- 2 cups broccoli florets, chopped
- 1 tomato, diced
- 1 tsp black pepper
- 1 tsp salt

Directions

1. Grease baking dish with butter and set aside.
2. Insert wire rack in rack position 6. Select bake, set temperature 390 F, timer for 20 minutes. Press start to preheat the oven.
3. In a bowl, whisk eggs, pepper, and salt. Add veggies and stir well.
4. Pour egg mixture into the baking dish and sprinkle with crumbled cheese.
5. Bake for 20 minutes.
6. Serve and enjoy.

Nutritional Value (Amount per Serving):
- Calories 214
- Fat 14.2 g
- Carbohydrates 5.4 g
- Sugar 2.6 g
- Protein 17.3 g
- Cholesterol 422 mg

Creamy Spinach Quiche

Prep Time	Cook Time	Serving
10 Minutes	35 Minutes	6

Ingredients

- 10 eggs
- 1 cup heavy cream
- 1 cup of coconut milk
- 1 tbsp butter
- 1 cup fresh spinach
- 1/4 cup fresh scallions, minced
- 1 cup cheddar cheese, shredded
- 1/4 tsp pepper
- 1/4 tsp salt

Directions

1. Spray 9*13-inch baking pan with cooking spray and set aside.
2. Insert wire rack in rack position 6. Select bake, set temperature 350 F, timer for 35 minutes. Press start to preheat the oven.
3. In a bowl, whisk eggs, cream, coconut milk, pepper, and salt.
4. Pour egg mixture into the baking pan and sprinkle with spinach, scallions, and cheese.
5. Bake for 35 minutes.
6. Serve and enjoy.

Nutritional Value (Amount per Serving):
- Calories 361
- Fat 32.4 g
- Carbohydrates 4.1 g
- Sugar 2.1 g
- Protein 15.5 g
- Cholesterol 325 mg

Crustleass Cheese Egg Quiche

Prep Time	Cook Time	Serving
10 Minutes	45 Minutes	8

Ingredients

- 12 eggs
- 8 oz cheddar cheese, grated
- 3/4 cup butter
- 4 oz cream cheese, softened
- Pepper
- Salt

Directions

1. Spray 10-inch pie pan with cooking spray and set aside.
2. Insert wire rack in rack position 6. Select bake, set temperature 375 F, timer for 20 minutes. Press start to preheat the oven.
3. Add half cup cheese into the pie pan.
4. Add eggs, cream cheese, and butter into the blender and blend until well combined.
5. Pour egg mixture in pie pan. Season with pepper and salt.
6. Sprinkle remaining cheese on top and bake for 45 minutes.
7. Serve and enjoy.

Nutritional Value (Amount per Serving):
- Calories 411
- Fat 38.2 g
- Carbohydrates 1.3 g
- Sugar 0.7 g
- Protein 16.6 g
- Cholesterol 337 mg

Mushroom Frittata

Prep Time	Cook Time	Serving
10 Minutes	20 Minutes	2

Ingredients

- 6 eggs
- 2 oz butter
- 2 oz scallions, chopped
- 3 oz fresh spinach
- 5 oz mushrooms, sliced
- 4 oz feta cheese, crumbled
- Pepper
- Salt

Directions

1. Spray a baking dish with cooking spray and set aside.
2. Insert wire rack in rack position 6. Select bake, set temperature 350 F, timer for 20 minutes. Press start to preheat the oven.
3. In a bowl, whisk eggs, cheese, pepper, and salt.
4. Melt butter in a pan over medium heat. Add mushrooms and scallions and sauté for 5-10 minutes.
5. Add spinach and sauté for 2 minutes. Transfer mushroom spinach mixture into the baking dish.
6. Pour egg mixture over mushroom spinach mixture and bake for 20 minutes.
7. Serve and enjoy.

Nutritional Value (Amount per Serving):
- Calories 576
- Fat 48.6 g
- Carbohydrates 9.3 g
- Sugar 5.4 g
- Protein 28.9 g
- Cholesterol 602 mg

Lemon Poppy Seed Donuts

Prep Time	Cook Time	Serving
10 Minutes	15 Minutes	8

Ingredients

- 4 eggs
- 2 tsp lemon zest
- 1/4 cup coconut oil, melted
- 1 tsp baking powder
- 1 tbsp poppy seeds
- 1/4 cup Swerve
- 1/2 tsp lemon extract
- 8 tbsp water
- 1/2 cup coconut flour
- 1/4 tsp salt

Directions

1. Spray donut pan with cooking spray and set aside.
2. Insert wire rack in rack position 6. Select bake, set temperature 350 F, timer for 15 minutes. Press start to preheat the oven.
3. In a mixing bowl, mix together coconut flour, baking powder, poppy seed, sweetener, and salt.
4. Stir in eggs, lemon extract, water, lemon zest, and melted oil until well combined.
5. Pour batter into the donut pan and bake for 15 minutes.
6. Serve and enjoy.

Nutritional Value (Amount per Serving):
- Calories 128
- Fat 10.2 g
- Carbohydrates 5.9 g
- Sugar 0.4 g
- Protein 4 g
- Cholesterol 82 mg

Artichoke Spinach Quiche

Prep Time	Cook Time	Serving
10 Minutes	40 Minutes	4

Ingredients

- 3 eggs
- 1 cup artichoke hearts, chopped
- 1 cup mushrooms, sliced
- 1 small onion, chopped
- 3 garlic cloves, minced
- 1/2 cup cottage cheese,
- 10 oz spinach, frozen
- 1 tsp olive oil
- Pepper
- Salt

Directions

1. Spray a pie dish with cooking spray and set aside.
2. Insert wire rack in rack position 6. Select bake, set temperature 350 F, timer for 40 minutes. Press start to preheat the oven.
3. Heat oil in a pan over medium heat. Add onion, mushrooms, garlic, and spinach and sauté for a minute.
4. In a mixing bowl, add cheese, artichoke hearts, eggs, pepper, and salt stir well. Add sautéed vegetables and stir well.
5. Pour egg mixture into the pie dish and bake for 40 minutes.
6. Serve and enjoy.

Nutritional Value (Amount per Serving):
- Calories 128
- Fat 5.4 g
- Carbohydrates 10.2 g
- Sugar 2 g
- Protein 12 g
- Cholesterol 125 mg

Coconut Zucchini Muffins

Prep Time	Cook Time	Serving
10 Minutes	25 Minutes	8

Ingredients

- 6 eggs
- 1/4 cup Swerve
- 1/3 cup coconut oil, melted
- 1 cup zucchini, grated
- 3/4 cup coconut flour
- 1/4 tsp ground nutmeg
- 1 tsp ground cinnamon
- 1/2 tsp baking soda

Directions

1. Spray 8 cups muffin pan with cooking spray and set aside.
2. Insert wire rack in rack position 6. Select bake, set temperature 350 F, timer for 25 minutes. Press start to preheat the oven.
3. Add all ingredients except zucchini in a bowl and mix well. Add zucchini and stir well.
4. Pour batter into the muffin pan and bake for 25 minutes.
5. Serve and enjoy.

Nutritional Value (Amount per Serving):
- Calories 174
- Fat 13.5 g
- Carbohydrates 8.5 g
- Sugar 0.5 g
- Protein 5.8 g
- Cholesterol 123 mg

Spicy Jalapeno Muffins

Prep Time	Cook Time	Serving
10 Minutes	20 Minutes	8

Ingredients

- 5 eggs
- 3 tbsp jalapenos, sliced
- 3 tbsp erythritol
- 2/3 cup coconut flour
- 1/4 cup coconut milk
- 1/3 cup coconut oil, melted
- 2 tsp baking powder
- 3/4 tsp sea salt

Directions

1. Spray 8 cups muffin pan with cooking spray and set aside.
2. Insert wire rack in rack position 6. Select bake, set temperature 350 F, timer for 20 minutes. Press start to preheat the oven.
3. In a large bowl, mix together coconut flour, baking powder, erythritol, and sea salt.
4. Stir in eggs, jalapenos, milk, and coconut oil until well combined.
5. Pour batter into the muffin pan and bake in for 20 minutes.
6. Serve and enjoy.

Nutritional Value (Amount per Serving):
- Calories 177
- Fat 14.6 g
- Carbohydrates 13.6 g
- Sugar 6.2 g
- Protein 5 g
- Cholesterol 102 mg

Spinach Egg Casserole

Prep Time	Cook Time	Serving
10 Minutes	35 Minutes	6

Ingredients

- 2 eggs
- 1 cup mushrooms, sliced
- 2 cups frozen spinach, thawed and drained
- 1 1/2 cups egg whites
- 1 1/4 cup cheddar cheese, shredded
- 1/2 red pepper, chopped
- 1/2 green pepper, chopped
- 1/2 onion, chopped
- Pepper
- Salt

Directions

1. Spray casserole dish with cooking spray and set aside.
2. Insert wire rack in rack position 6. Select bake, set temperature 375 F, timer for 35 minutes. Press start to preheat the oven.
3. Heat medium pan over medium-high heat.
4. Add chopped vegetables except spinach to the pan and sauté until vegetables are softened.
5. Add sauteed vegetables and spinach into the casserole dish.
6. In a bowl, whisk eggs, egg whites, pepper, and salt.
7. Pour egg mixture over the vegetables and sprinkle with shredded cheese.
8. Bake for 35 minutes.
9. Serve and enjoy.

Nutritional Value (Amount per Serving):

- Calories 161
- Fat 9.5 g
- Carbohydrates 3.7 g
- Sugar 2 g
- Protein 15.3 g
- Cholesterol 79 mg

Healthy Spinach Pie

Prep Time	Cook Time	Serving
10 Minutes	30 Minutes	6

Ingredients

- 5 eggs, beaten
- 10 oz frozen spinach, thawed, squeezed, and drained
- 1/4 tsp garlic powder
- 1 tsp dried onion, minced
- 2 1/2 cup cheddar cheese, grated
- Pepper
- Salt

Directions

1. Spray a 9-inch pie dish with cooking spray and set aside.
2. Insert wire rack in rack position 6. Select bake, set temperature 375 F, timer for 30 minutes. Press start to preheat the oven.
3. Add all ingredients into the mixing bowl and stir to combine.
4. Pour mixture into the pie dish and bake for 30 minutes.
5. Serve and enjoy.

Nutritional Value (Amount per Serving):

- Calories 254
- Fat 19.4 g
- Carbohydrates 2.8 g
- Sugar 0.8 g
- Protein 17.7 g
- Cholesterol 186 mg

Creamy Spinach Mushroom Quiche

Prep Time	Cook Time	Serving
10 Minutes	40 Minutes	6

Ingredients

- 6 eggs
- 1/2 tsp garlic powder
- 1 cup mozzarella cheese, shredded
- 1/3 cup parmesan cheese, shredded
- 8 oz can mushroom, sliced
- 10 oz frozen spinach, thawed and drained
- 1/2 cup water
- 1/2 cup heavy cream
- 2 cheese slices
- Pepper
- Salt

Directions

1. Insert wire rack in rack position 6. Select bake, set temperature 350 F, timer for 40 minutes. Press start to preheat the oven.
2. Spread spinach into a pie pan and spread mushrooms over spinach.
3. In a bowl, whisk eggs with water and heavy cream. Stir in garlic powder, parmesan, pepper, and salt.
4. Pour egg mixture into the pie pan. Top with mozzarella cheese.
5. Bake for 40 minutes.
6. Serve and enjoy.

Nutritional Value (Amount per Serving):
- Calories 184
- Fat 13.2 g
- Carbohydrates 4.2 g
- Sugar 0.7 g
- Protein 13 g
- Cholesterol 193 mg

Almond Butter Muffins

Prep Time	Cook Time	Serving
10 Minutes	15 Minutes	8

Ingredients

- 2 scoops vanilla protein powder
- 1/2 cup almond flour
- 1/2 cup coconut oil
- 1/2 cup pumpkin puree
- 1/2 cup almond butter
- 1 tbsp cinnamon
- 1 tsp baking powder

Directions

1. Spray 8 cups muffin pan with cooking spray and set aside.
2. Insert wire rack in rack position 6. Select bake, set temperature 350 F, timer for 15 minutes. Press start to preheat the oven.
3. In a large bowl, combine together all dry ingredients and mix well.
4. Add wet ingredients into the dry ingredients and stir to combine.
5. Pour batter into the muffin pan and bake for 15 minutes.
6. Serve and enjoy.

Nutritional Value (Amount per Serving):
- Calories 201
- Fat 17.6 g
- Carbohydrates 4.1 g
- Sugar 0.7 g
- Protein 8.7 g
- Cholesterol 0 mg

Bacon Egg Muffins

Prep Time	Cook Time	Serving
10 Minutes	25 Minutes	12

Ingredients

- 12 eggs
- 2 tbsp fresh parsley, chopped
- 1/2 tsp mustard powder
- 1/3 cup heavy cream
- 2 green onion, chopped
- 4 oz cheddar cheese, shredded
- 8 bacon slices, cooked and crumbled
- Pepper
- Salt

Directions

1. Spray 12 cups muffin pan with cooking spray and set aside.
2. Insert wire rack in rack position 6. Select bake, set temperature 375 F, timer for 25 minutes. Press start to preheat the oven.
3. In a mixing bowl, whisk eggs, mustard powder, heavy cream, pepper, and salt.
4. Divide cheddar cheese, onions, and bacon into the muffin cups then pour egg mixture into the muffin cups.
5. Bake for 25 minutes.
6. Serve and enjoy.

Nutritional Value (Amount per Serving):
- Calories 183
- Fat 14.1 g
- Carbohydrates 1 g
- Sugar 0.5 g
- Protein 12.8 g
- Cholesterol 192 mg

Zucchini Ham Quiche

Prep Time	Cook Time	Serving
10 Minutes	40 Minutes	6

Ingredients

- 8 eggs
- 1 cup cheddar cheese, shredded
- 1 cup zucchini, shredded and squeezed
- 1 cup ham, cooked and diced
- 1/2 tsp dry mustard
- 1/2 cup heavy cream
- Pepper
- Salt

Directions

1. Spray a 9-inch pie dish with cooking spray.
2. Insert wire rack in rack position 6. Select bake, set temperature 375 F, timer for 40 minutes. Press start to preheat the oven.
3. Mix ham, cheddar cheese, and zucchini in a pie dish.
4. In a bowl, whisk eggs, heavy cream, and seasoning.
5. Pour egg mixture over ham mixture.
6. Bake for 40 minutes.
7. Serve and enjoy.

Nutritional Value (Amount per Serving):
- Calories 235
- Fat 17.8 g
- Carbohydrates 2.6 g
- Sugar 0.9 g
- Protein 16.3 g
- Cholesterol 256 mg

Breakfast Egg Cups

Prep Time	Cook Time	Serving
10 Minutes	25 Minutes	12

Ingredients

- 12 eggs
- 4 oz cream cheese
- 12 bacon slices
- 1/4 cup buffalo sauce
- 2/3 cup cheddar cheese, shredded
- Pepper
- Salt

Directions

1. Spray 12 cups muffin pan with cooking spray and set aside.
2. Insert wire rack in rack position 6. Select bake, set temperature 375 F, timer for 20 minutes. Press start to preheat the oven.
3. Line each muffin cup with one bacon strip.
4. In a bowl, whisk eggs, pepper, and salt.
5. Pour egg mixture into each muffin cup and bake for 10 minutes.
6. In a separate bowl, mix together cheddar cheese and cream cheese and microwave for 30 seconds. Stir well and add buffalo sauce.
7. Remove muffin pan from oven and add 2 tsp cheese mixture in the center of each egg cup and bake for 15 minutes more.
8. Serve and enjoy.

Nutritional Value (Amount per Serving):

- Calories 224
- Fat 17.7 g
- Carbohydrates 1 g
- Sugar 0.4 g
- Protein 14.9 g
- Cholesterol 202 mg

Broccoli Muffins

Prep Time	Cook Time	Serving
10 Minutes	30 Minutes	6

Ingredients

- 2 eggs
- 2 cups almond flour
- 1 cup broccoli florets, chopped
- 1 tsp baking powder
- 2 tbsp nutritional yeast
- 1 cup almond milk
- 1/2 tsp sea salt

Directions

1. Spray 6-cups muffin pan with cooking spray and set aside.
2. Insert wire rack in rack position 6. Select bake, set temperature 350 F, timer for 30 minutes. Press start to preheat the oven.
3. Add all ingredients into the large bowl and whisk until well combined.
4. Pour egg mixture into the muffin pan and bake for 30 minutes.
5. Serve and enjoy.

Nutritional Value (Amount per Serving):

- Calories 355
- Fat 29 g
- Carbohydrates 13.3 g
- Sugar 1.7 g
- Protein 12.7 g
- Cholesterol 55 mg

Dijon Zucchini Gratin

Prep Time	Cook Time	Serving
10 Minutes	25 Minutes	4

Ingredients

- 1 egg, lightly beaten
- 1 1/4 cup unsweetened almond milk
- 3 medium zucchini, sliced
- 1 tbsp Dijon mustard
- 1/2 cup nutritional yeast
- 1 tsp sea salt

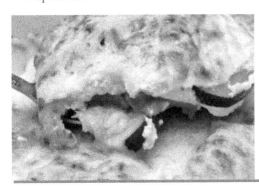

Directions

1. A spray casserole dish with cooking spray.
2. Insert wire rack in rack position 6. Select bake, set temperature 390 F, timer for 25 minutes. Press start to preheat the oven.
3. Arrange zucchini slices in a casserole dish.
4. In a saucepan, heat almond milk over low heat and stir in Dijon mustard, nutritional yeast, and sea salt. Add beaten egg and whisk well.
5. Pour sauce over zucchini slices and bake for 25 minutes.
6. Serve and enjoy.

Nutritional Value (Amount per Serving):
- Calories 125
- Fat 3.7 g
- Carbohydrates 15 g
- Sugar 2.7 g
- Protein 12.8 g
- Cholesterol 41 mg

Sausage Egg Muffins

Prep Time	Cook Time	Serving
10 Minutes	25 Minutes	12

Ingredients

- 6 eggs
- 1/2 red pepper, diced
- 1 cup egg whites
- 1 lb ground pork sausage
- 1/2 cup mozzarella cheese
- 1 cup cheddar cheese
- 3 tbsp onion, minced

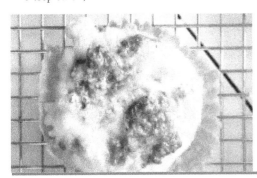

Directions

1. Spray 12-cups muffin pan with cooking spray and set aside.
2. Insert wire rack in rack position 6. Select bake, set temperature 350 F, timer for 25 minutes. Press start to preheat the oven.
3. Brown sausage in a pan over medium-high heat.
4. Divide red pepper, cheese, cooked sausages, and onion into each muffin cups.
5. In a large bowl, whisk together egg whites, egg, pepper, and salt.
6. Pour egg mixture into each muffin cups and bake for 25 minutes.
7. Serve and enjoy.

Nutritional Value (Amount per Serving):
- Calories 206
- Fat 15.6 g
- Carbohydrates 1.1 g
- Sugar 0.7 g
- Protein 14.4 g
- Cholesterol 126 mg

Cream Cheese Muffins

Prep Time	Cook Time	Serving
10 Minutes	20 Minutes	8

Ingredients

- 2 eggs
- 1/2 cup erythritol
- 8 oz cream cheese
- 1 tsp ground cinnamon
- 1/2 tsp vanilla

Directions

1. Spray 8-cups muffin pan with cooking spray and set aside.
2. Insert wire rack in rack position 6. Select bake, set temperature 350 F, timer for 20 minutes. Press start to preheat the oven.
3. In a bowl, mix together cream cheese, vanilla, erythritol, and eggs until soften.
4. Pour batter into the prepared muffin pan and sprinkle cinnamon on the top.
5. Bake for 20 minutes.
6. Serve and enjoy.

Nutritional Value (Amount per Serving):
- Calories 116
- Fat 11 g
- Carbohydrates 16.1 g
- Sugar 15.2 g
- Protein 3.5 g
- Cholesterol 72 mg

Sausage Egg Bake

Prep Time	Cook Time	Serving
10 Minutes	25 Minutes	8

Ingredients

- 6 eggs, lightly beaten
- 1 small onion, diced
- 1 lb sausage
- 1 cup cheddar cheese, shredded
- 1/2 tsp black pepper
- 1/2 tsp salt

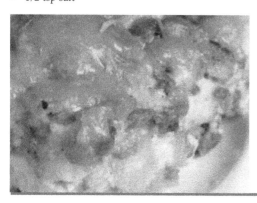

Directions

1. Insert wire rack in rack position 6. Select bake, set temperature 375 F, timer for 25 minutes. Press start to preheat the oven.
2. Brown onion and sausage in a pan over medium heat.
3. In a bowl, whisk eggs, cheese, pepper, and salt.
4. Add onion and sausage into the baking dish and pour the egg mixture on top.
5. Bake for 25 minutes.
6. Serve and enjoy.

Nutritional Value (Amount per Serving):
- Calories 300
- Fat 24.1 g
- Carbohydrates 1.3 g
- Sugar 0.7 g
- Protein 18.8 g
- Cholesterol 185 mg

Easy Cheese Pie

Prep Time	Cook Time	Serving
10 Minutes	25 Minutes	4

Ingredients

- 8 eggs
- 1 1/2 cups heavy whipping cream
- 1 lb cheddar cheese, grated
- Pepper
- Salt

Directions

1. Spray a pie dish with cooking spray and set aside.
2. Insert wire rack in rack position 6. Select bake, set temperature 350 F, timer for 25 minutes. Press start to preheat the oven.
3. In a bowl, whisk eggs, half cheese, heavy cream, pepper, and salt.
4. Sprinkle remaining cheese in prepared dish and bake for 5 minutes.
5. Remove dish from oven and let it cool slightly.
6. Now Pour egg mixture into the dish and bake 15-20 minutes.
7. Serve and enjoy.

Nutritional Value (Amount per Serving):

- Calories 738
- Fat 63 g
- Carbohydrates 3.4 g
- Sugar 1.3 g
- Protein 40.2 g
- Cholesterol 508 mg

Chapter 3 Poulltry Recipes

Chicken with Vegetables

Prep Time	Cook Time	Serving
10 Minutes	50 Minutes	4

Ingredients

- 8 chicken thighs, skinless and boneless
- 10 oz roasted red peppers, sliced
- 2 cups cherry tomatoes
- 1 1/2 lbs potatoes, cut into chunks
- 4 tbsp olive oil
- 1 tsp dried oregano
- 5 garlic cloves, crushed
- 1/4 cup capers, drained
- Pepper
- Salt

Directions

1. Insert wire rack in rack position 6. Select bake, set temperature 390 F, timer for 50 minutes. Press start to preheat the oven.
2. Season chicken with pepper and salt.
3. Heat 2 tablespoons of oil in a pan over medium-high heat. Add chicken and sear until brown from both the sides.
4. Place chicken in a roasting pan. Stir in potatoes, oregano, garlic, capers, red peppers, and tomatoes. Drizzle with olive oil.
5. Bake for 50 minutes.
6. Serve and enjoy.

Nutritional Value (Amount per Serving):
- Calories 837
- Fat 36.3 g
- Carbohydrates 36.7 g
- Sugar 7.6 g
- Protein 89.3 g
- Cholesterol 260 mg

Chicken Lasagna

Prep Time	Cook Time	Serving
10 Minutes	1 hour 5 Minutes	8

Ingredients

- 4 cups chicken, cooked and chopped
- 1 jar ragu cheese sauce
- 1 tsp garlic salt
- 10 oz frozen spinach, thawed, drained, and chopped
- 16 oz chive and onion cream cheese
- 12 lasagna noodles, cooked
- 3 cups mozzarella cheese, shredded

Directions

1. Spray a 9*13-inch baking dish with cooking spray and set aside.
2. Insert wire rack in rack position 6. Select bake, set temperature 350 F, timer for 50 minutes. Press start to preheat the oven.
3. In a bowl, stir together chicken, garlic salt, spinach, and cream cheese.
4. Spread 1/3 tomato sauce in a baking dish then place 4 noodles, 1/3 chicken, and 1 cup cheese. Repeat layer twice.
5. Cover dish with foil and bake for 50 minutes. Remove foil and bake for 15 minutes more.
6. Serve and enjoy.

Nutritional Value (Amount per Serving):
- Calories 708
- Fat 33.3 g
- Carbohydrates 57.7 g
- Sugar 3.4 g
- Protein 38 g
- Cholesterol 174 mg

Bacon Chicken Lasagna

Prep Time	Cook Time	Serving
10 Minutes	25 Minutes	8

Ingredients

- 3 cups chicken, cooked and shredded
- 2 1/2 cups mozzarella cheese, grated
- 3/4 lb bacon, cooked and crumbled
- 1/2 cup sun-dried tomatoes, chopped
- 14 oz artichoke hearts, drained and chopped
- 1/2 cup parmesan cheese, grated
- 12 lasagna noodles, cooked
- 3 tbsp ranch dressing
- 1 1/4 cups milk
- 16 oz cream cheese

Directions

1. Spray a 9*13-inch baking dish with cooking spray and set aside.
2. Insert wire rack in rack position 6. Select bake, set temperature 350 F, timer for 25 minutes. Press start to preheat the oven.
3. In a bowl, mix together chicken, tomatoes, artichokes, parmesan cheese, 1 cup mozzarella cheese, and bacon.
4. In a separate bowl, mix together milk, ranch dressing, and cream cheese.
5. Pour half milk mixture over the chicken and stir well. Pour half milk mixture in the baking dish.
6. Place 3 lasagna noodles in the baking dish then place 1/3 chicken mixture and half cup mozzarella cheese. Repeat layers twice.
7. Bake for 25 minutes.
8. Serve and enjoy.

Nutritional Value (Amount per Serving):
- Calories 851
- Fat 44.3 g
- Carbohydrates 60 g
- Sugar 2.8 g
- Protein 53.1 g
- Cholesterol 191 mg

Delicious Mexican Chicken Lasagna

Prep Time	Cook Time	Serving
10 Minutes	15 Minutes	15

Ingredients

- 1 1/2 lbs chicken breast, cooked and shredded
- 2 tsp ground cumin
- 2 tbsp chili powder
- 1 cup of salsa
- 3/4 cup sour cream
- 2 cup cheese, shredded
- 4 tortillas
- 1 tsp dry onion, minced

Directions

1. Insert wire rack in rack position 6. Select bake, set temperature 390 F, timer for 15 minutes. Press start to preheat the oven.
2. Mix together chicken, dried onion, cumin, chili powder, salsa, and sour cream.
3. Spray baking dish with cooking spray.
4. Spread half chicken mixture in a baking dish then place 2 tortillas on top.
5. Sprinkle 1/2 cheese over the tortillas then repeat the layers.
6. Bake for 15 minutes.
7. Serve and enjoy.

Nutritional Value (Amount per Serving):
- Calories 160
- Fat 9 g
- Carbohydrates 5.3 g
- Sugar 0.8 g
- Protein 14.5 g
- Cholesterol 50 mg

Pumpkin Chicken Lasagna

Prep Time	Cook Time	Serving
10 Minutes	35 Minutes	8

Ingredients

- 1 lb chicken, boneless and chopped
- 1 tsp olive oil
- 1 cup milk
- 14 oz can cream of pumpkin soup
- 1 1/2 cups mozzarella cheese, shredded
- 9 lasagna noodles
- 16 oz pasta sauce

Directions

1. Insert wire rack in rack position 6. Select bake, set temperature 390 F, timer for 35 minutes. Press start to preheat the oven.
2. In a bowl, combine together soup and milk. Set aside.
3. Heat oil in a saucepan over medium heat.
4. Add chicken in a saucepan and sauté until cooked.
5. Stir in pasta sauce and simmer for 15 minutes.
6. Spread 1/3 sauce mixture into the baking dish then place 3 noodles and top with 1/3 soup mixture. Repeat layers twice. Sprinkle cheese over noodles.
7. Bake for 35 minutes.
8. Serve and enjoy.

Nutritional Value (Amount per Serving):
- Calories 597
- Fat 10.9 g
- Carbohydrates 77.6 g
- Sugar 11.9 g
- Protein 45.1 g
- Cholesterol 116 mg

Cheesy Chicken Lasagna

Prep Time	Cook Time	Serving
10 Minutes	45 Minutes	9

Ingredients

- 3 cups chicken, cooked and diced
- 1/2 cup onion, chopped
- 8 lasagna noodles, cooked and drained
- 1/2 cup green bell pepper, chopped
- 1/2 cup parmesan cheese, grated
- 1/2 Tsp dried basil
- 2 cups processed cheese, shredded
- 16 oz cottage cheese
- 6 oz can mushroom, drained and sliced
- 10 oz can cream of chicken soup
- 1/4 cup pimento peppers, chopped
- 3/4 cup milk
- 3 tbsp butter

Directions

1. Insert wire rack in rack position 6. Select bake, set temperature 350 F, timer for 45 minutes. Press start to preheat the oven.
2. Melt butter in a saucepan over medium heat. Add bell pepper, onion and sauté.
3. Stir in soup, pimento, basil, processed cheese, milk, and mushrooms.
4. Place 1/2 noodles in a baking dish then layer with 1/2 cream sauce, half cottage cheese, half chicken, and half parmesan cheese. Repeat layers.
5. Bake for 45 minutes.
6. Serve and enjoy.

Nutritional Value (Amount per Serving):
- Calories 449
- Fat 16.8 g
- Carbohydrates 38.8 g
- Sugar 3.8 g
- Protein 35 g
- Cholesterol 96 mg

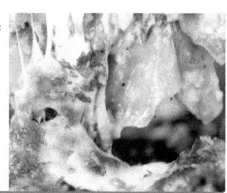

Parmesan Chicken & Veggies

Prep Time	Cook Time	Serving
10 Minutes	30 Minutes	4

Ingredients

- 4 chicken breasts, skinless and boneless
- 2 tbsp olive oil
- 1/2 tsp garlic powder
- 1/2 cup Parmesan cheese, grated
- 1/2 cup Italian seasoned breadcrumbs
- 4 tbsp butter, melted
- 1/2 lb baby potatoes cut into fourths
- 1 yellow squash, sliced
- 1 zucchini, sliced
- Pepper
- Salt

Directions

1. Spray a baking dish with cooking spray and set aside.
2. Insert wire rack in rack position 6. Select bake, set temperature 350 F, timer for 30 minutes. Press start to preheat the oven.
3. Place melted butter in a shallow dish.
4. In another dish mix together, parmesan cheese, breadcrumbs, and garlic powder.
5. Season chicken with pepper and salt then dip into the melted butter and coat with cheese mixture.
6. Place coated chicken in a baking dish.
7. In mixing bowl, add potatoes, yellow squash, zucchini, and olive oil toss well.
8. Add vegetables into the baking dish around the chicken and bake for 30 minutes.
9. Serve and enjoy.

Nutritional Value (Amount per Serving):
- Calories 579
- Fat 32.7 g
- Carbohydrates 20.4 g
- Sugar 2.3 g
- Protein 50.2 g
- Cholesterol 169 mg

Chicken Cheese Rice

Prep Time	Cook Time	Serving
10 Minutes	25 Minutes	4

Ingredients

- 1 cup chicken breast, cooked and shredded
- 2 tbsp all-purpose flour
- 2 cup cooked brown rice
- 1 tbsp garlic, minced
- 2 tbsp butter
- 1 cup cheddar cheese, shredded
- 1 cup chicken stock
- 1/2 tbsp fresh thyme, chopped
- 1/2 tsp pepper
- 1/1 tsp salt

Directions

1. Spray a baking dish with cooking spray and set aside.
2. Insert wire rack in rack position 6. Select bake, set temperature 350 F, timer for 25 minutes. Press start to preheat the oven.
3. Melt butter in a pan over medium-high heat. Add garlic and cook for 1 minute. Add thyme, pepper, salt, and flour stir well.
4. Pour chicken stock into the pan and whisk constantly. Whisk until thick then add cheese and stir until melted.
5. Add chicken and cooked rice stir well to combine. Transfer pan mixture into the baking dish and bake for 25 minutes.
6. Serve and enjoy.

Nutritional Value (Amount per Serving):
- Calories 559
- Fat 18.5 g
- Carbohydrates 77 g
- Sugar 0.4 g
- Protein 20.3 g
- Cholesterol 61 mg

Lemon Rosemary Chicken

Prep Time	Cook Time	Serving
10 Minutes	25 Minutes	2

Ingredients

- 2 chicken breasts, boneless and skinless
- 1 garlic clove, minced
- 1 spring rosemary, chopped
- 1 tbsp rosemary leaves
- 12 oz small potatoes, halved
- 1/2 tbsp olive oil
- 1 lemon juice
- 1 tsp red chili flakes
- Salt

Directions

1. Insert wire rack in rack position 6. Select bake, set temperature 390 F, timer for 25 minutes. Press start to preheat the oven.
2. Add potatoes into the boiling water and cook for 10 minutes. Drain well and set aside.
3. In a bowl, place chicken and add spring rosemary, garlic, chili flakes, lemon juice, rosemary leaves, and olive oil mix well.
4. In a pan, place chicken over medium-high heat for 5 minutes.
5. Transfer chicken in a baking tray and add potatoes in-tray.
6. Place the tray in oven and roast chicken for 25 minutes.
7. Serve and enjoy.

Nutritional Value (Amount per Serving):
- Calories 446
- Fat 15.5 g
- Carbohydrates 29.2 g
- Sugar 2.7 g
- Protein 46 g
- Cholesterol 132 mg

Spicy Chicken Wings

Prep Time	Cook Time	Serving
10 Minutes	30 Minutes	4

Ingredients

- 2 lbs fresh chicken wings
- 4 tbsp cayenne pepper sauce
- 2 tbsp spring onion, chopped
- 1 tbsp brown sugar
- 1 tbsp Worcestershire sauce
- 4 tbsp butter
- 1 tsp sea salt

Directions

1. Line roasting pan with foil and set aside.
2. Insert wire rack in rack position 6. Select bake, set temperature 350 F, timer for 30 minutes. Press start to preheat the oven.
3. Arrange chicken wings on roasting pan and bake for 30 minutes.
4. In a large bowl, mix together brown sugar, Worcestershire sauce, butter, cayenne pepper sauce, and salt.
5. Remove wings from oven and place in sauce bowl toss well until all wings are coated well with the sauce.
6. Garnish with chopped spring onion.
7. Serve and enjoy.

Nutritional Value (Amount per Serving):
- Calories 563
- Fat 29.3 g
- Carbohydrates 6.2 g
- Sugar 3.6 g
- Protein 66.4 g
- Cholesterol 132 mg

Olive Tomato Chicken

Prep Time	Cook Time	Serving
10 Minutes	22 Minutes	4

Ingredients

- 4 chicken breast, boneless and halves
- 15 olives, pitted and halved
- 2 cups cherry tomatoes
- 3 tbsp olive oil
- 3 tbsp capers, rinsed and drained
- Pepper
- Salt

Directions

1. Insert wire rack in rack position 6. Select bake, set temperature 390 F, timer for 20 minutes. Press start to preheat the oven.
2. In a bowl, toss tomatoes, capers, olives with 2 tablespoons of oil. Set aside.
3. Season chicken with pepper and salt.
4. Heat remaining oil in a pan over high heat.
5. Place chicken in the pan and cook for 4 minutes.
6. Transfer chicken onto the roasting pan and top with tomato mixture and bake for 20 minutes.
7. Serve and enjoy.

Nutritional Value (Amount per Serving):
- Calories 241
- Fat 15 g
- Carbohydrates 4.9 g
- Sugar 2.4 g
- Protein 22.3 g
- Cholesterol 64 mg

Chicken Paillard

Prep Time	Cook Time	Serving
10 Minutes	25 Minutes	8

Ingredients

- 4 chicken breasts, skinless and boneless
- 1/2 cup olives, diced
- 1 small onion, sliced
- 1 fennel bulb, sliced
- 28 oz can tomatoes, diced
- 1/4 cup fresh basil, chopped
- 1/4 cup fresh parsley, chopped
- 1/4 cup pine nuts
- 2 tbsp olive oil
- Pepper
- Salt

Directions

1. Insert wire rack in rack position 6. Select bake, set temperature 390 F, timer for 25 minutes. Press start to preheat the oven.
2. Arrange chicken in baking dish and season with pepper and salt and drizzle with oil.
3. In a bowl, mix together olives, tomatoes, pine nuts, onion, fennel, pepper, and salt.
4. Pour olive mixture over chicken and bake for 25 minutes.
5. Garnish with basil and parsley.
6. Serve and enjoy.

Nutritional Value (Amount per Serving):
- Calories 242
- Fat 12.8 g
- Carbohydrates 9.3 g
- Sugar 3.9 g
- Protein 23.2 g
- Cholesterol 65 mg

Juicy Garlic Chicken

Prep Time	Cook Time	Serving
10 Minutes	40 Minutes	6

Ingredients

- 2 lbs chicken thighs, skinless and boneless
- 8 garlic cloves, sliced
- 2 tbsp olive oil
- 2 tbsp fresh parsley, chopped
- 1 fresh lemon juice
- Pepper
- Salt

Directions

1. Insert wire rack in rack position 6. Select bake, set temperature 390 F, timer for 40 minutes. Press start to preheat the oven.
2. Place chicken on roasting pan and season with pepper and salt.
3. Sprinkle parsley and garlic over the chicken and drizzle with oil and lemon juice.
4. Bake for 40 minutes.
5. Serve and enjoy.

Nutritional Value (Amount per Serving):
- Calories 336
- Fat 16 g
- Carbohydrates 1.6 g
- Sugar 0.2 g
- Protein 44.1 g
- Cholesterol 135 mg

Lemon Pepper Chicken

Prep Time	Cook Time	Serving
10 Minutes	35 Minutes	4

Ingredients

- 4 chicken thighs
- 1 tsp garlic powder
- 1 tbsp lemon pepper seasoning
- 2 tbsp fresh lemon juice
- 1/2 tsp paprika
- 1/2 tsp Italian seasoning
- 1/2 tsp onion powder
- 2 tbsp olive oil
- 1 tsp salt

Directions

1. Insert wire rack in rack position 6. Select bake, set temperature 390 F, timer for 35 minutes. Press start to preheat the oven.
2. Add chicken in the large bowl.
3. Mix together lemon juice and olive oil and pour over chicken.
4. Mix together paprika, Italian seasoning, onion powder, garlic powder, lemon pepper seasoning, and salt and rub all over the chicken.
5. Arrange chicken on a roasting pan and bake for 35 minutes.
6. Serve and enjoy.

Nutritional Value (Amount per Serving):
- Calories 338
- Fat 17.7 g
- Carbohydrates 2.2 g
- Sugar 0.5 g
- Protein 40.9 g
- Cholesterol 125 mg

Spicy Chicken Meatballs

Prep Time	Cook Time	Serving
10 Minutes	25 Minutes	4

Ingredients

- 1 lb ground chicken
- 1/2 cup cilantro, chopped
- 1 jalapeno pepper, minced
- 1 habanero pepper, minced
- 1 poblano chili pepper, minced
- Salt

Directions

1. Insert wire rack in rack position 4. Select air fry, set temperature 400 F, timer for 25 minutes. Press start to preheat the oven.
2. Add all ingredients into the large bowl and mix until well combined.
3. Make small balls from meat mixture and place on an air fryer basket and air fry for 25 minutes.
4. Serve and enjoy.

Nutritional Value (Amount per Serving):
- Calories 226
- Fat 8.5 g
- Carbohydrates 2.3 g
- Sugar 0.7 g
- Protein 33.4 g
- Cholesterol 101 mg

Turkey Meatballs

Prep Time	Cook Time	Serving
10 Minutes	20 Minutes	6

Ingredients

- 1 lb ground turkey
- 1 tbsp basil, chopped
- 1/3 cup coconut flour
- 2 cups zucchini, grated
- 1 tsp dried oregano
- 1 tbsp garlic, minced
- 1 tsp cumin
- 1 tbsp dried onion flakes
- 2 eggs, lightly beaten
- 1 tbsp nutritional yeast
- Pepper
- Salt

Directions

1. Insert wire rack in rack position 6. Select bake, set temperature 390 F, timer for 20 minutes. Press start to preheat the oven.
2. Add all ingredients into the mixing bowl and mix until well combined.
3. Make small balls from meat mixture and place on a roasting pan and bake for 20 minutes.
4. Serve and enjoy.

Nutritional Value (Amount per Serving):
- Calories 214
- Fat 10.7 g
- Carbohydrates 8.1 g
- Sugar 1.1 g
- Protein 24.9 g
- Cholesterol 132 mg

Tandoori Chicken

Prep Time	Cook Time	Serving
10 Minutes	15 Minutes	4

Ingredients

- 1 lb chicken tenders, cut in half
- 1/4 cup parsley, chopped
- 1 tbsp garlic, minced
- 1 tbsp ginger, minced
- 1/4 cup yogurt
- 1 tsp paprika
- 1 tsp garam masala
- 1 tsp turmeric
- 1 tsp cayenne pepper
- 1 tsp salt

Directions

1. Insert wire rack in rack position 4. Select air fry, set temperature 350 F, timer for 15 minutes. Press start to preheat the oven.
2. Add all ingredients into the large bowl and mix well. Place in refrigerator for 30 minutes.
3. Add marinated chicken into the air fryer basket and cook for 15 minutes.
4. Serve and enjoy.

Nutritional Value (Amount per Serving):
- Calories 240
- Fat 8.9 g
- Carbohydrates 3.9 g
- Sugar 1.3 g
- Protein 34.2 g
- Cholesterol 102 mg

Hot Chicken Wings

Prep Time	Cook Time	Serving
10 Minutes	25 Minutes	4

Ingredients

- 2 lbs chicken wings
- 1/2 tsp Worcestershire sauce
- 1/2 tsp Tabasco
- 6 tbsp butter, melted
- 12 oz hot sauce

Directions

1. Insert wire rack in rack position 4. Select air fry, set temperature 380 F, timer for 25 minutes. Press start to preheat the oven.
2. Add chicken wings into the air fryer basket and cook for 25 minutes.
3. Meanwhile, in a bowl, mix together hot sauce, Worcestershire sauce, and butter. Set aside.
4. Add cooked chicken wings into the sauce bowl and toss well.
5. Serve and enjoy.

Nutritional Value (Amount per Serving):
- Calories 594
- Fat 34.4 g
- Carbohydrates 1.6 g
- Sugar 1.2 g
- Protein 66.2 g
- Cholesterol 248 mg

Garlicky Chicken Wings

Prep Time	Cook Time	Serving
10 Minutes	20 Minutes	4

Ingredients

- 12 chicken wings
- 1 tbsp chili powder
- 1/2 tbsp baking powder
- 1 tsp granulated garlic
- 1/2 tsp sea salt

Directions

1. Insert wire rack in rack position 4. Select air fry, set temperature 410 F, timer for 20 minutes. Press start to preheat the oven.
2. Add chicken wings into the large bowl and toss with remaining ingredients.
3. Transfer chicken wings into the air fryer basket and air fry for 20 minutes.
4. Serve and enjoy.

Nutritional Value (Amount per Serving):

- Calories 580
- Fat 22.6 g
- Carbohydrates 2.4 g
- Sugar 0.3 g
- Protein 87.1 g
- Cholesterol 267 mg

Fajita Chicken

Prep Time	Cook Time	Serving
10 Minutes	15 Minutes	4

Ingredients

- 4 chicken breasts, make horizontal cuts on each piece
- 2 tbsp fajita seasoning
- 2 tbsp olive oil
- 1 onion, sliced
- 1 bell pepper, sliced

Directions

1. Insert wire rack in rack position 4. Select air fry, set temperature 380 F, timer for 15 minutes. Press start to preheat the oven.
2. Rub oil and seasoning all over the chicken breast.
3. Place chicken into the air fryer basket and top with bell peppers and onion.
4. Cook for 15 minutes.
5. Serve and enjoy.

Nutritional Value (Amount per Serving):

- Calories 374
- Fat 17.9 g
- Carbohydrates 8 g
- Sugar 2.7 g
- Protein 42.8 g
- Cholesterol 130 mg

Yummy Chicken Tenders

Prep Time	Cook Time	Serving
10 Minutes	12 Minutes	4

Ingredients

- 1 lb chicken tenderloin
- 1/3 cup breadcrumb
- 3 eggs, lightly beaten
- 2 tbsp olive oil
- 1/2 cup all-purpose flour
- Pepper
- Salt

Directions

1. Insert wire rack in rack position 4. Select air fry, set temperature 330 F, timer for 12 minutes. Press start to preheat the oven.
2. In a shallow dish, mix together flour, pepper, and salt. Add breadcrumbs in a separate shallow dish. Add egg in a small bowl.
3. Roll chicken in flour then dips in egg and coat with breadcrumbs.
4. Place coated chicken on roasting pan and air fry for 12 minutes.
5. Serve and enjoy.

Nutritional Value (Amount per Serving):
- Calories 296
- Fat 11.5 g
- Carbohydrates 18.7 g
- Sugar 0.9 g
- Protein 29.9 g
- Cholesterol 171 mg

Old Bay Chicken Wings

Prep Time	Cook Time	Serving
10 Minutes	45 Minutes	4

Ingredients

- 3 lbs chicken wings
- 1 tbsp old bay seasoning
- 2 tsp xanthan gum
- 1 tsp fresh lemon juice
- 1/2 cup butter, melted

Directions

1. Insert wire rack in rack position 4. Select air fry, set temperature 360 F, timer for 45 minutes. Press start to preheat the oven.
2. Add chicken wings, xanthan gum, and old bay seasoning to the large bowl and toss well.
3. Transfer chicken wings to the air fryer basket and air fry for 45 minutes.
4. In a large bowl mix together melted butter and lemon juice.
5. Add cooked chicken wings to the butter lemon mixture and toss well.
6. Serve and enjoy.

Nutritional Value (Amount per Serving):
- Calories 853
- Fat 48.2 g
- Carbohydrates 4.1 g
- Sugar 0.1 g
- Protein 99 g
- Cholesterol 364 mg

Chinese Chicken Wings

Prep Time	Cook Time	Serving
10 Minutes	30 Minutes	2

Ingredients

- 4 chicken wings
- 1 tsp mixed spice
- 1 tbsp soy sauce
- 1 tbsp Chinese spice
- Pepper
- Salt

Directions

1. Insert wire rack in rack position 4. Select air fry, set temperature 350 F, timer for 30 minutes. Press start to preheat the oven.
2. Add chicken wings into the bowl. Add remaining ingredients and toss well.
3. Transfer chicken wings into the air fryer basket and air fry for 15 minutes.
4. Serve and enjoy.

Nutritional Value (Amount per Serving):
- Calories 429
- Fat 17.3 g
- Carbohydrates 2.1 g
- Sugar 0.6 g
- Protein 62.4 g
- Cholesterol 178 mg

Chicken Kabab

Prep Time	Cook Time	Serving
10 Minutes	6 Minutes	3

Ingredients

- 1 lb ground chicken
- 1/4 cup almond flour
- 2 green onion, chopped
- 1 egg, lightly beaten
- 1/3 cup fresh parsley, chopped
- 2 garlic cloves
- 4 oz onion, chopped
- 1/4 tsp turmeric powder
- 1/2 tsp black pepper
- 1 tbsp fresh lemon juice

Directions

1. Insert wire rack in rack position 4. Select air fry, set temperature 400 F, timer for 6 minutes. Press start to preheat the oven.
2. Add all ingredients into the food processor and process until well combined.
3. Transfer chicken mixture to the bowl and place it in the refrigerator for 30 minutes.
4. Divide mixture into the 6 equal portions and roll around the soaked wooden skewers.
5. Place kabab into the air fryer basket air fry for 6 minutes.
6. Serve and enjoy.

Nutritional Value (Amount per Serving):
- Calories 391
- Fat 17.3 g
- Carbohydrates 7.9 g
- Sugar 2.1 g
- Protein 48.6 g
- Cholesterol 189 mg

Caribbean Chicken

Prep Time	Cook Time	Serving
10 Minutes	10 Minutes	8

Ingredients

- 3 lbs chicken thigh, skinless and boneless
- 1 tbsp cayenne
- 1 tbsp cinnamon
- 1 tbsp coriander powder
- 3 tbsp coconut oil, melted
- 1/2 tsp ground nutmeg
- 1/2 tsp ground ginger
- Pepper
- Salt

Directions

1. Insert wire rack in rack position 4. Select air fry, set temperature 390 F, timer for 10 minutes. Press start to preheat the oven.
2. In a small bowl, mix together all ingredients except chicken.
3. Rub bowl mixture all over the chicken.
4. Place chicken into the air fryer basket and air fry for 10 minutes.
5. Serve and enjoy.

Nutritional Value (Amount per Serving):

- Calories 373
- Fat 17.9 g
- Carbohydrates 1.2 g
- Sugar 0.1 g
- Protein 49.3 g
- Cholesterol 151 mg

Chicken Coconut Meatballs

Prep Time	Cook Time	Serving
10 Minutes	10 Minutes	4

Ingredients

- 1 lb ground chicken
- 1 tbsp soy sauce
- 1 tbsp hoisin sauce
- 1/2 cup fresh cilantro, chopped
- 2 green onions, chopped
- 1/4 cup shredded coconut
- 1 tsp sesame oil
- 1 tsp sriracha
- Pepper
- Salt

Directions

1. Insert wire rack in rack position 4. Select air fry, set temperature 350 F, timer for 10 minutes. Press start to preheat the oven.
2. Add all ingredients into the large bowl and mix until well combined.
3. Make small balls and place them into the air fryer basket and air fry for 10 minutes.
4. Serve and enjoy.

Nutritional Value (Amount per Serving):

- Calories 258
- Fat 11.4 g
- Carbohydrates 3.7 g
- Sugar 1.7 g
- Protein 33.5 g
- Cholesterol 101 mg

Chapter 4 Meat Recipes

Tender Pork Chops

Prep Time	Cook Time	Serving
10 Minutes	13 Minutes	4

Ingredients

- 4 pork chops, boneless
- 1/2 tsp celery seeds
- 1/2 tsp parsley
- 1/2 tsp granulated onion
- 1/2 tsp granulated garlic
- 2 tsp olive oil
- 1/2 tsp salt

Directions

1. Insert wire rack in rack position 4. Select air fry, set temperature 350 F, timer for 13 minutes. Press start to preheat the oven.
2. In a small bowl, mix together with seasonings and sprinkle onto the pork chops.
3. Place pork chops into the air fryer basket and cook for 13 minutes.
4. Serve and enjoy.

Nutritional Value (Amount per Serving):
- Calories 278
- Fat 22.3 g
- Carbohydrates 0.4 g
- Sugar 0.1 g
- Protein 18.1 g
- Cholesterol 69 mg

Simple Dash Seasoned Pork Chops

Prep Time	Cook Time	Serving
10 Minutes	20 Minutes	2

Ingredients

- 2 pork chops, boneless
- 1 tbsp dash seasoning

Directions

1. Insert wire rack in rack position 4. Select air fry, set temperature 360 F, timer for 20 minutes. Press start to preheat the oven.
2. Rub seasoning all over the pork chops.
3. Place seasoned pork chops into the air fryer basket and cook for 20 minutes.
4. Serve and enjoy.

Nutritional Value (Amount per Serving):
- Calories 256
- Fat 19.9 g
- Carbohydrates 0 g
- Sugar 0 g
- Protein 18 g
- Cholesterol 69 mg

Jerk Pork Butt

Prep Time	Cook Time	Serving
10 Minutes	20 Minutes	4

Ingredients

- 1 1/2 lbs pork butt, cut into pieces
- 1/4 cup jerk paste

Directions

1. Insert wire rack in rack position 4. Select air fry, set temperature 390 F, timer for 20 minutes. Press start to preheat the oven.
2. Add meat and jerk paste into the bowl and coat well. Place in refrigerator overnight.
3. Place marinated meat into the air fryer basket and cook for 20 minutes.
4. Serve and enjoy.

Nutritional Value (Amount per Serving):
- Calories 339
- Fat 12.1 g
- Carbohydrates 0.8 g
- Sugar 0.6 g
- Protein 53 g
- Cholesterol 156 mg

Asian Lamb

Prep Time	Cook Time	Serving
10 Minutes	10 Minutes	4

Ingredients

- 1 lb lamb, cut into 2-inch pieces
- 1 tbsp soy sauce
- 2 tbsp vegetable oil
- 1/2 tsp cayenne
- 1 1/2 tbsp ground cumin
- 2 red chili peppers, chopped
- 1 tbsp garlic, minced
- 1 tsp salt

Directions

1. Insert wire rack in rack position 4. Select air fry, set temperature 360 F, timer for 10 minutes. Press start to preheat the oven.
2. Mix together cumin and cayenne in a small bowl. Rub meat with cumin mixture and place in a large bowl.
3. Add oil, soy sauce, garlic, chili peppers, and salt over the meat. Coat well and place it in the refrigerator overnight.
4. Add marinated meat to the air fryer basket and cook for 10 minutes.
5. Serve and enjoy.

Nutritional Value (Amount per Serving):
- Calories 286
- Fat 15.7 g
- Carbohydrates 2.3 g
- Sugar 0.3 g
- Protein 32.7 g
- Cholesterol 102 mg

Beef Stew

Prep Time	Cook Time	Serving
10 Minutes	5 hours	8

Ingredients

- 3 lbs beef stew meat, trimmed
- 1/2 cup Thai red curry paste
- 1/3 cup tomato paste
- 13 oz can coconut milk
- 2 tsp ginger, minced
- 2 garlic cloves, minced
- 1 medium onion, sliced
- 2 tbsp extra virgin olive oil
- 2 cups carrots, julienned
- 2 cups broccoli florets
- 2 tsp fresh lime juice
- 2 tbsp fish sauce
- 2 tsp sea salt

Directions

1. Insert wire rack in rack position 8. Select slow cook, Set HIGH for 5 hours. Press start to preheat the oven.
2. Heat 1 tbsp oil in a pan over medium-high heat. Add meat and brown the meat on all sides.
3. Transfer brown meat into the dutch oven.
4. Add remaining oil in a pan and sauté ginger, garlic, and onion over medium-high heat for 5 minutes. Add coconut milk and stir well.
5. Transfer pan mixture into the dutch oven.
6. Add remaining ingredients except for carrots and broccoli into the dutch oven.
7. Cover the dutch oven and cook on high for 5 hours.
8. Add carrots and broccoli during the last 30 minutes of cooking.
9. Serve and enjoy.

Nutritional Value (Amount per Serving):
- Calories 537
- Fat 28.6 g
- Carbohydrates 13 g
- Protein 54.4 g
- Cholesterol 152 mg

Mushroom Beef Stew

Prep Time	Cook Time	Serving
10 Minutes	8 hours	6

Ingredients

- 3 lbs stewing steak, cut into pieces
- 4 cups mushrooms, quartered
- 1 tbsp Worcestershire sauce
- 2 tbsp tomato paste
- 1 1/4 cup beef stock
- 2 tbsp parsley, chopped
- 1 tbsp thyme leaves
- 1 bay leaf
- 3 medium carrots, peeled and cut into chunks
- Pepper
- Salt

Directions

1. Insert wire rack in rack position 8. Select slow cook, Set LOW for 8 hours. Press start to preheat the oven.
2. Add beef, thyme, bay leaf, carrots, and mushrooms to the dutch oven.
3. Whisk together beef stock, Worcestershire sauce, and tomato paste and pour into the dutch oven. Season beef mixture with pepper and salt. Stir well.
4. Cover and cook on low for 8 hours.
5. Garnish with parsley and serve.

Nutritional Value (Amount per Serving):
- Calories 399
- Fat 15.3 g
- Carbohydrates 6.4 g
- Protein 57.5 g
- Cholesterol 0 mg

Spicy Pepper Beef

Prep Time	Cook Time	Serving
10 Minutes	4 hours	6

Ingredients

- 2 lbs beef chuck, sliced
- 1 cup beef broth
- 1/2 medium onion, sliced
- 2 cups bell pepper, chopped
- 1 tbsp sriracha sauce
- 1/3 cup parsley, chopped
- 2 tsp garlic powder
- 1 tsp black pepper
- 2 tsp salt

Directions

1. Insert wire rack in rack position 8. Select slow cook, Set HIGH for 4 hours. Press start to preheat the oven.
2. Place meat into the dutch oven.
3. Top meat with sliced onion and bell pepper. Season with garlic powder, pepper, and salt.
4. Mix together sriracha and broth and pour over meat mixture.
5. Cover and cook on high for 4 hours.
6. Garnish with chopped parsley and serve.

Nutritional Value (Amount per Serving):
- Calories 325
- Fat 11.5 g
- Carbohydrates 5.3 g
- Protein 47.5 g
- Cholesterol 137 mg

Slow Cooked Beef Brisket

Prep Time	Cook Time	Serving
10 Minutes	7 hours	6

Ingredients

- 3 lbs beef brisket
- 1 tbsp chili powder
- 4 garlic cloves, chopped
- 1/2 onion, chopped
- 1 tsp cumin
- 3 tbsp chili sauce
- 1/4 cup beef broth
- 1 1/2 tsp liquid smoke
- 1 tbsp Worcestershire sauce
- 1/2 tsp black pepper

Directions

1. Insert wire rack in rack position 8. Select slow cook, Set LOW for 7 hours. Press start to preheat the oven.
2. Mix together chili powder, pepper, cumin, Worcestershire sauce, and garlic and rub over brisket.
3. Place the beef brisket into the dutch oven. Mix together broth, chili sauce, onion, and liquid smoke and pour over brisket.
4. Cover and cook on low for 7 hours.
5. Remove brisket from dutch oven and cut into slices.
6. Serve and enjoy.

Nutritional Value (Amount per Serving):
- Calories 439
- Fat 14.5 g
- Carbohydrates 3.1 g
- Protein 69.5 g
- Cholesterol 203 mg

Slow Cooked Pork Chops

Prep Time	Cook Time	Serving
10 Minutes	6 hours	4

Ingredients

- 4 pork chops
- 1 1/2 cups chicken broth
- 2 tbsp butter, melted
- 3 garlic cloves, minced
- 1 medium onion, chopped
- 3/4 tsp poultry seasoning
- 1/2 tsp salt

Directions

1. Insert wire rack in rack position 8. Select slow cook, Set LOW for 6 hours. Press start to preheat the oven.
2. In a large bowl, mix together butter, broth, and poultry seasoning and salt.
3. Pour bowl mixture into the dutch oven.
4. Add pork chops, onion, and garlic into the dutch oven.
5. Cover and cook on low for 6 hours.
6. Serve and enjoy.

Nutritional Value (Amount per Serving):
- Calories 337
- Fat 26.2 g
- Carbohydrates 3.8 g
- Protein 20.3 g
- Cholesterol 84 mg

Cuban Pork

Prep Time	Cook Time	Serving
10 Minutes	8 hours	6

Ingredients

- 3 lbs pork shoulder roast
- 1/4 tsp red pepper flakes, crushed
- 1 tsp dried oregano
- 1 tsp cumin
- 1/2 cup fresh lime juice
- 1 bay leaf
- 1 small onion, sliced
- 6 garlic cloves, minced
- 1/8 tsp black pepper
- 1/2 cup orange juice
- 2 tbsp olive oil
- 1 1/2 tsp salt

Directions

1. Insert wire rack in rack position 8. Select slow cook, Set LOW for 8 hours. Press start to preheat the oven.
2. In a bowl, whisk together garlic, pepper, red pepper flakes, oregano, cumin, salt, lime juice, orange juice, and oil.
3. Pierce pork with knife and rub with garlic mixture.
4. Place pork into the dutch oven with bay leaf and onion.
5. Cover and cook on low for 8 hours.
6. Remove pork from Dutch oven and shred using the pork.
7. Serve and enjoy.

Nutritional Value (Amount per Serving):
- Calories 645
- Fat 51 g
- Carbohydrates 4.8 g
- Protein 38.7 g
- Cholesterol 161 mg

Steak Bites

Prep Time	Cook Time	Serving
10 Minutes	8 hours	4

Ingredients

- 3 lbs round steak, cut into cubes
- 1/2 cup beef broth, low sodium
- 4 tbsp butter, sliced
- 1 tsp garlic powder
- 1 tbsp onion, minced
- 1/2 tsp black pepper
- 1/2 tsp salt

Directions

1. Insert wire rack in rack position 8. Select slow cook, Set LOW for 8 hours. Press start to preheat the oven.
2. Add steak cubes into the dutch oven. Pour beef broth over the meat.
3. Sprinkle garlic powder, onion, pepper and salt over the meat.
4. Top with butter slices. Cover and cook on low for 8 hours.
5. Serve and enjoy.

Nutritional Value (Amount per Serving):
- Calories 845
- Fat 44.4 g
- Carbohydrates 1 g
- Protein 103.6 g
- Cholesterol 320 mg

Pot Roast

Prep Time	Cook Time	Serving
10 Minutes	8 hours 30 Minutes	12

Ingredients

- 3 lbs chuck roast, boneless
- 1 onion, quartered
- 4 celery stalks, sliced
- 1/2 cup beef broth
- 1 tsp garlic powder
- 1 tsp pepper

Directions

1. Insert wire rack in rack position 8. Select slow cook, Set LOW for 8 hours. Press start to preheat the oven.
2. Mix together garlic powder, pepper, and salt and rub over the chuck roast.
3. Heat a few tablespoons of oil in a pan. Sear the meat in the pan from all sides.
4. Add meat, broth, and vegetables into the dutch oven.
5. Cover and cook on low for 8 hours.
6. Shred the meat using a fork and cook for 30 minutes more.
7. Serve and enjoy.

Nutritional Value (Amount per Serving):
- Calories 252
- Fat 9.5 g
- Carbohydrates 1.4 g
- Protein 37.8 g
- Cholesterol 115 mg

Flank Steak

Prep Time	Cook Time	Serving
10 Minutes	8 hours	8

Ingredients

- 3 lbs flank steak
- 1 large onion, chopped
- 1 large carrot, chopped
- 1/2 cup water
- 1 bay leaf
- 1/4 tsp dried thyme
- Pepper
- Salt

Directions

1. Insert wire rack in rack position 8. Select slow cook, Set HIGH for 8 hours. Press start to preheat the oven.
2. Season steak with pepper and salt.
3. Place season steak into the dutch oven.
4. Add onion and carrot over the steak.
5. Add thyme, bay leaves, and water over the steak.
6. Cover and cook on high for 8 hours.
7. Serve and enjoy.

Nutritional Value (Amount per Serving):
- Calories 292
- Fat 14 g
- Carbohydrates 2 g
- Protein 36 g
- Cholesterol 70 mg

Delicious Pork Carnitas

Prep Time	Cook Time	Serving
10 Minutes	8 hours	6

Ingredients

- 3 lbs pork chops. boneless
- 2 garlic cloves, minced
- 1 red pepper, sliced
- 1 yellow pepper, sliced
- 1 onion, diced
- 1/2 cup water
- 1/2 cup taco sauce
- 2 bay leaves
- 1 tbsp cumin
- 2 tbsp chili powder
- Pepper
- Salt

Directions

1. Insert wire rack in rack position 8. Select slow cook, Set LOW for 8 hours. Press start to preheat the oven.
2. Pour water into the dutch oven.
3. Add pork chops into the dutch oven.
4. Add all remaining ingredients over the pork chops and stir well.
5. Cover and cook on low for 8 hours.
6. Using fork shred the meat.
7. Serve and enjoy.

Nutritional Value (Amount per Serving):
- Calories 482
- Fat 16 g
- Carbohydrates 9.1 g
- Protein 72.2 g
- Cholesterol 209 mg

Flavors Caesar Pork Chops

Prep Time	Cook Time	Serving
10 Minutes	8 hours 30 Minutes	5

Ingredients

- 2 lbs pork chops
- 10.5 oz Caesar dressing
- 1/4 tsp pepper
- Salt

Directions

1. Insert wire rack in rack position 8. Select slow cook, Set LOW for 8 hours. Press start to preheat the oven.
2. Season chops with pepper and salt.
3. Place seasoned pork chops into the dutch oven.
4. Sprinkle caesar dressing over the pork chops.
5. Cover and cook over low for 8 hours.
6. Serve and enjoy.

Nutritional Value (Amount per Serving):
- Calories 580
- Fat 43.8 g
- Carbohydrates 10.5 g
- Protein 34.4 g
- Cholesterol 131 mg

Beef Pot Roast

Prep Time	Cook Time	Serving
10 Minutes	8 hours	2

Ingredients

- 8 oz beef chuck roast
- 15 baby carrots, sliced
- 3 small potatoes, cut into cubed
- 1/2 packet onion soup mix
- 1/2 medium onion, sliced

Directions

1. Insert wire rack in rack position 8. Select slow cook, Set LOW for 8 hours. Press start to preheat the oven.
2. Place carrots and potatoes into the bottom of the dutch oven.
3. Place meat on top of veggies than add remaining ingredients.
4. Cover and cook on low for 8 hours.
5. Serve and enjoy.

Nutritional Value (Amount per Serving):
- Calories 630
- Fat 32 g
- Carbohydrates 50 g
- Sugar 7.8 g
- Protein 34.9 g
- Cholesterol 117 mg

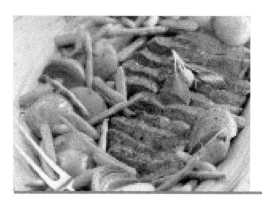

Korean Beef

Prep Time	Cook Time	Serving
10 Minutes	4 hours	2

Ingredients

- 1 lb flank steak, cut into strips
- 1/4 cup soy sauce
- 1/4 tsp garlic, minced
- 1 tbsp sesame oil
- 2 tbsp cornstarch
- 1/8 tsp red pepper flakes
- 1/2 small onion, chopped
- 6 tbsp brown sugar
- 1/4 cup beef broth

Directions

1. Insert wire rack in rack position 8. Select slow cook, Set LOW for 4 hours. Press start to preheat the oven.
2. Add cornstarch and flank steak pieces into the ziplock bag and shake well to coat.
3. Add remaining ingredients into the dutch oven and stir well.
4. Add coated steak pieces into the dutch oven. Stir well.
5. Cover and cook on low for 4 hours.
6. Serve and enjoy.

Nutritional Value (Amount per Serving):
- Calories 663
- Fat 25.9 g
- Carbohydrates 38.1 g
- Sugar 27.6 g
- Protein 66 g
- Cholesterol 125 mg

Spicy Jalapeno Beef

Prep Time	Cook Time	Serving
10 Minutes	6 hours	2

Ingredients

- 1 lb beef chuck roast
- 1/2 onion, sliced
- 1/4 cup Worcestershire sauce
- 1/4 cup beef broth
- 6 oz jar roasted bell peppers, drained and chopped
- 2 jalapenos, sliced
- 1/4 tsp black pepper
- 1/2 tsp salt

Directions

1. Insert wire rack in rack position 8. Select slow cook, Set LOW for 6 hours. Press start to preheat the oven.
2. Place chuck roast into the dutch oven.
3. Pour Worcestershire sauce and beef broth over the roast. Season with pepper and salt.
4. Top roast with bell peppers, jalapenos, and sliced onions.
5. Cover and cook on low for 6 hours.
6. Shred the meat using a fork.
7. Serve and enjoy.

Nutritional Value (Amount per Serving):
- Calories 1299
- Fat 83.8 g
- Carbohydrates 65.8 g
- Sugar 11.1 g
- Protein 65.6 g
- Cholesterol 234 mg

Shredded Beef

Prep Time	Cook Time	Serving
10 Minutes	6 hours	2

Ingredients

- 1 lb beef chuck shoulder roast, boneless and fat trimmed
- 2 banana peppers, seed discarded and sliced
- 1 cup beef broth
- 1/2 medium onion, sliced

Directions

1. Insert wire rack in rack position 8. Select slow cook, Set LOW for 6 hours. Press start to preheat the oven.
2. Add all ingredients into the dutch oven.
3. Cover and cook on low for 6 hours.
4. Shred the meat using a fork.
5. Serve and enjoy.

Nutritional Value (Amount per Serving):
- Calories 490
- Fat 27.1 g
- Carbohydrates 12 g
- Sugar 7.5 g
- Protein 46.1 g
- Cholesterol 151 mg

Meatloaf

Prep Time	Cook Time	Serving
10 Minutes	20 Minutes	4

Ingredients

- 1 lb ground pork
- 1 onion, chopped
- 1 tbsp thyme, chopped
- 1/4 tsp garlic powder
- 1 egg, lightly beaten
- 3 tbsp breadcrumbs
- Pepper
- Salt

Directions

1. Spray a loaf pan with cooking spray and set aside.
2. Insert wire rack in rack position 6. Select bake, set temperature 390 F, timer for 20 minutes. Press start to preheat the oven.
3. Add all ingredients into the mixing bowl and mix until well combined.
4. Pour meat mixture into the loaf pan and bake for 20 minutes.
5. Serve and enjoy.

Nutritional Value (Amount per Serving):
- Calories 211
- Fat 5.4 g
- Carbohydrates 6.9 g
- Sugar 1.6 g
- Protein 32.1 g
- Cholesterol 124 mg

Meatballs

Prep Time	Cook Time	Serving
10 Minutes	12 Minutes	4

Ingredients

- 1 egg, lightly beaten
- 1 tbsp oregano, chopped
- 4 oz ground lamb meat
- 1/2 tbsp lemon zest
- Pepper
- Salt

Directions

1. Line baking tray with parchment paper and set aside.
2. Insert wire rack in rack position 6. Select bake, set temperature 390 F, timer for 12 minutes. Press start to preheat the oven.
3. Add all ingredients into the bowl and mix until well combined.
4. Make small balls from meat mixture and place them on a baking tray and bake for 12 minutes.
5. Serve and enjoy.

Nutritional Value (Amount per Serving):
- Calories 77
- Fat 5 g
- Carbohydrates 1 g
- Sugar 0.2 g
- Protein 6.8 g
- Cholesterol 61 mg

Italian Meatballs

Prep Time	Cook Time	Serving
10 Minutes	20 Minutes	4

Ingredients

- 1 lb ground beef
- 1/2 small onion, chopped
- 1 egg, lightly beaten
- 2 garlic cloves, minced
- 1 tbsp basil, chopped
- 1/4 cup parmesan cheese, grated
- 1/2 cup breadcrumbs
- 1 tbsp Italian parsley, chopped
- 1 tbsp rosemary, chopped
- 2 tbsp milk
- Pepper
- Salt

Directions

1. Insert wire rack in rack position 6. Select bake, set temperature 375 F, timer for 20 minutes. Press start to preheat the oven.
2. Add all ingredients into the bowl and mix until well combined.
3. Make small balls from meat mixture and place them on a baking tray and cook for 20 minutes.
4. Serve and enjoy.

Nutritional Value (Amount per Serving):
- Calories 311
- Fat 10.4 g
- Carbohydrates 12.3 g
- Sugar 1.7 g
- Protein 39.9 g
- Cholesterol 147 mg

Cheesy Baked Patties

Prep Time	Cook Time	Serving
10 Minutes	15 Minutes	6

Ingredients

- 2 lbs ground beef
- 1 cup mozzarella cheese, grated
- 1 tsp onion powder
- 1 tsp garlic powder
- Pepper
- Salt

Directions

1. Insert wire rack in rack position 6. Select bake, set temperature 390 F, timer for 15 minutes. Press start to preheat the oven.
2. Add all ingredients into the large bowl and mix until well combined.
3. Make patties from meat mixture and place on a baking tray and bake for 15 minutes.
4. Serve and enjoy.

Nutritional Value (Amount per Serving):

- Calories 297
- Fat 10.3 g
- Carbohydrates 0.8 g
- Sugar 0.3 g
- Protein 47.3 g
- Cholesterol 138 mg

Lamb Meatballs

Prep Time	Cook Time	Serving
10 Minutes	15 Minutes	4

Ingredients

- 1 lb ground lamb
- 1 tsp onion powder
- 1 tbsp garlic, minced
- 1 tsp ground coriander
- 1 tsp ground cumin
- Pepper
- Salt

Directions

1. Insert wire rack in rack position 6. Select bake, set temperature 390 F, timer for 15 minutes. Press start to preheat the oven.
2. Add all ingredients into the large bowl and mix until well combined.
3. Make small balls from the meat mixture and place them on a baking tray and bake for 15 minutes.
4. Serve and enjoy.

Nutritional Value (Amount per Serving):

- Calories 218
- Fat 8.5 g
- Carbohydrates 1.4 g
- Sugar 0.2 g
- Protein 32.1 g
- Cholesterol 102 mg

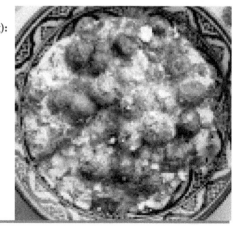

Crispy Crusted Pork Chops

Prep Time	Cook Time	Serving
10 Minutes	30 Minutes	3

Ingredients

- 3 pork chops, boneless
- 3 tbsp parmesan cheese, grated
- 1/2 cup crushed crackers
- 2 tbsp milk
- 1 egg, lightly beaten
- Pepper
- Salt

Directions

1. Spray a baking dish with cooking spray and set aside.
2. Insert wire rack in rack position 6. Select bake, set temperature 350 F, timer for 30 minutes. Press start to preheat the oven.
3. In a shallow bowl, whisk egg and milk.
4. In a separate shallow dish, mix together cheese, crackers, pepper, and salt.
5. Dip pork chops in egg then coat with cheese mixture and place in a baking dish and bake for 30 minutes.
6. Serve and enjoy.

Nutritional Value (Amount per Serving):
- Calories 320
- Fat 23.7 g
- Carbohydrates 3.3 g
- Sugar 1.1 g
- Protein 22.3 g
- Cholesterol 128 mg

Meatballs

Prep Time	Cook Time	Serving
10 Minutes	20 Minutes	6

Ingredients

- 8 oz ground beef
- 1/2 onion, diced
- 1 egg, lightly beaten
- 1/4 cup parmesan cheese, grated
- 1/2 cup breadcrumbs
- 1/4 cup parsley, chopped
- 1 tsp garlic, minced
- 8 oz ground pork
- Pepper
- Salt

Directions

1. Insert wire rack in rack position 6. Select bake, set temperature 390 F, timer for 20 minutes. Press start to preheat the oven.
2. Add all ingredients into the large bowl and mix until well combined.
3. Make small balls from meat mixture and place them on a baking tray and bake for 20 minutes.
4. Serve and enjoy.

Nutritional Value (Amount per Serving):
- Calories 188
- Fat 5.7 g
- Carbohydrates 7.9 g
- Sugar 1 g
- Protein 24.9 g
- Cholesterol 91 mg

Tasty Crispy Crust Pork Chops

Prep Time	Cook Time	Serving
10 Minutes	15 Minutes	2

Ingredients

- 2 pork chops, bone-in
- 1 tbsp olive oil
- 1 cup crushed pork rinds
- 1/2 tsp garlic powder
- 1/2 tsp onion powder
- 1/2 tsp paprika
- 1/2 tsp parsley

Directions

1. Insert wire rack in rack position 6. Select air fry, set temperature 400 F, timer for 15 minutes. Press start to preheat the oven.
2. In a large bowl, mix together pork rinds, garlic powder, onion powder, parsley, and paprika.
3. Brush pork chops with oil and coat with pork rind mixture and place on an air fryer basket and cook for 15 minutes.
4. Serve and enjoy.

Nutritional Value (Amount per Serving):
- Calories 362
- Fat 29.5 g
- Carbohydrates 1.3 g
- Sugar 0.4 g
- Protein 22.8 g
- Cholesterol 79 mg

Meatballs

Prep Time	Cook Time	Serving
10 Minutes	20 Minutes	6

Ingredients

- 1 lb ground beef
- 1 tbsp fresh rosemary, chopped
- 1/2 small onion, minced
- 2 garlic cloves, minced
- 1/4 cup parmesan cheese, grated
- 1/2 cup breadcrumbs
- 1 egg, lightly beaten
- 1 tbsp fresh basil, chopped
- 1 tbsp fresh parsley, chopped
- Pepper
- Salt

Directions

1. Insert wire rack in rack position 6. Select bake, set temperature 375 F, timer for 20 minutes. Press start to preheat the oven.
2. Add all ingredients into the mixing bowl and mix until well combined.
3. Make small balls from meat mixture and place them on a baking tray and bake for 20 minutes.
4. Serve and enjoy.

Nutritional Value (Amount per Serving):
- Calories 205
- Fat 6.8 g
- Carbohydrates 8 g
- Sugar 0.9 g
- Protein 26.4 g
- Cholesterol 98 mg

Lemon Pepper Pork Chops

Prep Time	Cook Time	Serving
10 Minutes	15 Minutes	4

Ingredients

- 4 pork chops, boneless
- 1 tsp lemon pepper seasoning
- Salt

Directions

1. Insert wire rack in rack position 6. Select air fry, set temperature 400 F, timer for 15 minutes. Press start to preheat oven
2. Season pork chops with lemon pepper seasoning, and salt and place on an air fryer basket and cook for 15 minutes.
3. Serve and enjoy.

Nutritional Value (Amount per Serving):
- Calories 257
- Fat 19.9 g
- Carbohydrates 0.3 g
- Sugar 0 g
- Protein 18 g
- Cholesterol 69 mg

Delicious Pork Patties

Prep Time	Cook Time	Serving
10 Minutes	35 Minutes	6

Ingredients

- 2 lbs ground pork
- 1 egg, lightly beaten
- 1 onion, minced
- 1 carrot, minced
- 1/2 cup breadcrumbs
- 1 tsp garlic powder
- 1 tsp paprika
- Pepper
- Salt

Directions

1. Insert wire rack in rack position 6. Select bake, set temperature 375 F, timer for 30 minutes. Press start to preheat the oven.
2. Add all ingredients into the large bowl and mix until well combined.
3. Make small patties from meat mixture and place on a baking tray and cook for 20 minutes.
4. Turn patties bake for 15 minutes more.
5. Serve and enjoy.

Nutritional Value (Amount per Serving):
- Calories 276
- Fat 6.6 g
- Carbohydrates 9.8 g
- Sugar 2.1 g
- Protein 42.1 g
- Cholesterol 138 mg

Lamb Chops

Prep Time	Cook Time	Serving
10 Minutes	30 Minutes	4

Ingredients

- 4 lamb chops
- 1 1/2 tsp tarragon
- 1 1/2 tsp ginger
- 1/4 cup brown sugar
- 1 tsp garlic powder
- 1 tsp ground cinnamon
- Pepper
- Salt

Directions

1. Insert wire rack in rack position 6. Select bake, set temperature 375 F, timer for 30 minutes. Press start to preheat the oven.
2. Add garlic powder, cinnamon, tarragon, ginger, brown sugar, pepper, and salt into the zip-lock bag and mix well.
3. Add lamb chops in a zip-lock bag. The sealed bag shakes well and places it in the refrigerator for 2 hours.
4. Place marinated lamb chops on a roasting pan and bake for 30 minutes.
5. Serve and enjoy.

Nutritional Value (Amount per Serving):
- Calories 650
- Fat 24.1 g
- Carbohydrates 10.5 g
- Sugar 9 g
- Protein 92.1 g
- Cholesterol 294 mg

Meatballs

Prep Time	Cook Time	Serving
10 Minutes	15 Minutes	4

Ingredients

- 1 lb ground pork
- 1/2 tsp dried thyme
- 1 tsp paprika
- 1 tsp garlic powder
- 1/2 tsp ground cumin
- 1/2 tsp coriander
- 1 tsp onion powder
- Pepper
- Salt

Directions

1. Insert wire rack in rack position 6. Select bake, set temperature 390 F, timer for 15 minutes. Press start to preheat the oven.
2. Add all ingredients into the large bowl and mix until well combined.
3. Make small balls from the meat mixture and place them on a baking tray and bake for 15 minutes.
4. Serve and enjoy.

Nutritional Value (Amount per Serving):
- Calories 170
- Fat 4.1 g
- Carbohydrates 1.5 g
- Sugar 0.4 g
- Protein 30 g
- Cholesterol 83 mg

Ranch Pork Chops

Prep Time	Cook Time	Serving
10 Minutes	35 Minutes	6

Ingredients

- 6 pork chops, boneless
- 1 oz ranch seasoning
- 2 tbsp olive oil
- 1 tsp dried parsley

Directions

1. Line baking tray with parchment paper and set aside.
2. Insert wire rack in rack position 6. Select bake, set temperature 390 F, timer for 35 minutes. Press start to preheat the oven.
3. Mix together oil, dried parsley, and ranch seasoning and rub over pork chops.
4. Place pork chops on a baking tray and cook for 35 minutes.
5. Serve and enjoy.

Nutritional Value (Amount per Serving):
- Calories 311
- Fat 24.6 g
- Carbohydrates 0 g
- Sugar 0 g
- Protein 18 g
- Cholesterol 69 mg

Country Style Baked Pork Chops

Prep Time	Cook Time	Serving
10 Minutes	35 Minutes	2

Ingredients

- 2 pork chops
- 2 onion sliced
- 2 tbsp ketchup
- 2 tbsp brown sugar
- Pepper
- Salt

Directions

1. Insert wire rack in rack position 6. Select bake, set temperature 375 F, timer for 35 minutes. Press start to preheat the oven.
2. Season pork chops with pepper and salt.
3. Place pork chops in a baking dish. Mix together ketchup and brown sugar and pour over pork chops.
4. Top with onion slices. Cover baking dish with foil and bake for 35 minutes.
5. Serve and enjoy.

Nutritional Value (Amount per Serving):
- Calories 308
- Fat 19.9 g
- Carbohydrates 13.5 g
- Sugar 12.5 g
- Protein 18.2 g
- Cholesterol 69 mg

Baked Patties

Prep Time	Cook Time	Serving
10 Minutes	15 Minutes	4

Ingredients

- 1 lb ground lamb
- 1 tsp ground coriander
- 1 tsp ground cumin
- 1/4 cup fresh parsley, chopped
- 1/4 cup onion, minced
- 1/4 tsp cayenne pepper
- 1/2 tsp ground allspice
- 1 tsp ground cinnamon
- 1 tbsp garlic, minced
- 1/4 tsp pepper
- 1 tsp kosher salt

Directions

1. Insert wire rack in rack position 6. Select bake, set temperature 390 F, timer for 15 minutes. Press start to preheat the oven.
2. Add all ingredients into the large bowl and mix until well combined.
3. Make small balls from meat mixture and place on a baking tray and lightly flatten the meatballs with back on spoon.
4. Bake for 15 minutes.
5. Serve and enjoy.

Nutritional Value (Amount per Serving):
- Calories 223
- Fat 8.5 g
- Carbohydrates 2.6 g
- Sugar 0.4 g
- Protein 32.3 g
- Cholesterol 102 mg

Lamb Roast

Prep Time	Cook Time	Serving
10 Minutes	8 hours	8

Ingredients

- 4 lbs lamb roast, boneless
- 4 garlic cloves, cut into slivers
- 1 tsp oregano
- 1/4 tsp pepper
- 1/2 tsp marjoram
- 1/2 tsp thyme
- 2 tsp salt

Directions

1. Insert wire rack in rack position 8. Select slow cook, Set LOW for 8 hours. Press start to preheat the oven.
2. Using a sharp knife make small cuts all over lamb roast then insert garlic slivers into the cuts.
3. In a small bowl, mix together marjoram, thyme, oregano, pepper, and salt and rub all over lamb roast.
4. Place lamb roast into the dutch oven.
5. Cover and cook on low for 8 hours.
6. Serve and enjoy.

Nutritional Value (Amount per Serving):
- Calories 605
- Fat 48.2 g
- Carbohydrates 0.7 g
- Sugar 0 g
- Protein 38.3 g
- Cholesterol 161 mg

Italian Pork Roast

Prep Time	Cook Time	Serving
10 Minutes	6 hours	8

Ingredients

- 2 lbs lean pork roast, boneless
- 1 tbsp parsley
- 1/2 cup parmesan cheese, grated
- 28 oz can tomatoes, diced
- 1 tsp dried oregano
- 1 tsp dried basil
- 1 tsp garlic powder
- Pepper
- Salt

Directions

1. Insert wire rack in rack position 8. Select slow cook, Set LOW for 6 hours. Press start to preheat the oven.
2. Add the meat into the dutch oven.
3. Mix together tomatoes, oregano, basil, garlic powder, parsley, cheese, pepper, and salt and pour over meat.
4. Cover and cook on low for 6 hours.
5. Serve and enjoy.

Nutritional Value (Amount per Serving):
- Calories 237
- Fat 8.4 g
- Carbohydrates 5.7 g
- Sugar 3.5 g
- Protein 33.7 g
- Cholesterol 94 mg

Meatballs

Prep Time	Cook Time	Serving
10 Minutes	20 Minutes	4

Ingredients

- 1 lb ground lamb
- 3 tbsp olive oil
- 1/4 tsp red pepper flakes
- 1 tbsp garlic, minced
- 1 egg, lightly beaten
- 1 tsp ground cumin
- 2 tsp fresh oregano, chopped
- 2 tbsp fresh parsley, chopped
- 1/4 tsp pepper
- 1 tsp kosher salt

Directions

1. Line baking tray with parchment paper.
2. Insert wire rack in rack position 6. Select bake, set temperature 390 F, timer for 20 minutes. Press start to preheat the oven.
3. Add all ingredients except oil into the mixing bowl and mix until well combined.
4. Make small meatballs from meat mixture and place on a prepared baking tray.
5. Drizzle oil over meatballs and bake in for 20 minutes.
6. Serve and enjoy.

Nutritional Value (Amount per Serving):
- Calories 325
- Fat 20.2 g
- Carbohydrates 1.7 g
- Sugar 0.2 g
- Protein 33.6 g
- Cholesterol 143 mg

Garlicky Beef Roast

Prep Time	Cook Time	Serving
10 Minutes	8 hours	6

Ingredients

- 2 lbs lean top round beef roast
- 1 tbsp Italian seasoning
- 6 garlic cloves, minced
- 1 onion, sliced
- 2 cups beef broth
- 1/2 cup red wine
- 1 tsp red pepper flakes
- Pepper
- Salt

Directions

1. Insert wire rack in rack position 8. Select slow cook, Set LOW for 8 hours. Press start to preheat the oven.
2. Season meat with pepper and salt and place into the dutch oven.
3. Pour remaining ingredients over meat.
4. Cover and cook on low for 8 hours.
5. Remove meat from dutch oven and shred using a fork.
6. Return shredded meat to the dutch oven and stir well.
7. Serve and enjoy.

Nutritional Value (Amount per Serving):
- Calories 231
- Fat 6.7 g
- Carbohydrates 4 g
- Sugar 1.4 g
- Protein 35.8 g
- Cholesterol 76 mg

Tender Pork Tenderloin

Prep Time	Cook Time	Serving
10 Minutes	15 Minutes	4

Ingredients

- 1 1/2 lbs pork tenderloin
- 1 tsp garlic powder
- 1 tsp Italian seasoning
- 2 tbsp olive oil
- 1 tsp ground coriander
- 1/4 tsp pepper
- 1 tsp sea salt

Directions

1. Insert wire rack in rack position 6. Select bake, set temperature 390 F, timer for 15 minutes. Press start to preheat the oven.
2. Rub pork tenderloin with 1 tablespoon of olive oil.
3. Mix together coriander, garlic powder, Italian seasoning, pepper, and salt and rub over pork tenderloin.
4. Heat remaining oil in a pan over medium-high heat.
5. Add pork tenderloin in hot oil and cook until brown from all the sides.
6. Place pork tenderloin on a baking tray and cook for 15 minutes.
7. Slice and serve.

Nutritional Value (Amount per Serving):
- Calories 310
- Fat 13.3 g
- Carbohydrates 0.7 g
- Sugar 0.3 g
- Protein 44.7 g
- Cholesterol 125 mg

Creole Pork Chops

Prep Time	Cook Time	Serving
10 Minutes	10 Minutes	6

Ingredients

- 6 pork chops, boneless
- 2 tbsp Creole mustard
- 1/2 cup zesty Italian dressing
- 1 tbsp Italian seasoning

Directions

1. Insert wire rack in rack position 6. Select bake, set temperature 375 F, timer for 30 minutes. Press start to preheat the oven.
2. Add pork chops in a mixing bowl.
3. Pour remaining ingredients over pork chops and coat well and place them in the refrigerator for 30 minutes.
4. Arrange marinated pork chops on a baking tray and cook 10 minutes or until internal temperature reaches 145 F.
5. Serve and enjoy.

Nutritional Value (Amount per Serving):
- Calories 280
- Fat 21.8 g
- Carbohydrates 0.5 g
- Sugar 0.4 g
- Protein 18 g
- Cholesterol 70 mg

Delicious Burger Patties

Prep Time	Cook Time	Serving
10 Minutes	12 Minutes	4

Ingredients

- 1 lb ground beef
- 1/4 tsp red pepper flakes
- 1/2 tsp garlic powder
- 1/2 tsp onion powder
- Pepper
- Salt

Directions

1. Insert wire rack in rack position 6. Select bake, set temperature 350 F, timer for 12 minutes. Press start to preheat the oven.
2. Add all ingredients into the mixing bowl and mix until well combined.
3. Make four patties from meat mixture and place on a baking tray and bake for 12 minutes.
4. Serve and enjoy.

Nutritional Value (Amount per Serving):
- Calories 213
- Fat 7.1 g
- Carbohydrates 0.6 g
- Sugar 0.2 g
- Protein 34.5 g
- Cholesterol 101 mg

Meatballs

Prep Time	Cook Time	Serving
10 Minutes	10 Minutes	4

Ingredients

- 1 egg
- 1 lb ground beef
- 2 tbsp taco seasoning
- 1 tbsp garlic, minced
- 1/4 cup cilantro, chopped
- 1/4 cup onion, chopped
- 1/2 cup cheddar cheese, shredded
- Pepper
- Salt

Directions

1. Insert wire rack in rack position 6. Select bake, set temperature 390 F, timer for 10 minutes. Press start to preheat the oven.
2. Add ground beef and remaining ingredients into the mixing bowl and mix until well combined.
3. Make small meatballs and place them on a baking tray and bake for 10 minutes.
4. Serve and enjoy.

Nutritional Value (Amount per Serving):
- Calories 293
- Fat 13 g
- Carbohydrates 1.9 g
- Sugar 0.5 g
- Protein 39.7 g
- Cholesterol 158 mg

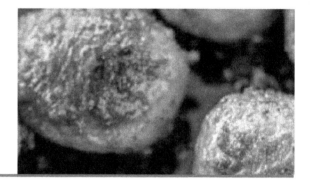

Creamy Pork Chops

Prep Time	Cook Time	Serving
10 Minutes	6 hours	4

Ingredients

- 4 pork chops, boneless
- 2 chicken bouillon cubes, crushed
- 1 cup milk
- 10 oz can cream chicken soup
- 10 oz can cream mushrooms soup
- 1/2 tsp dried basil
- 1 tsp onion powder
- 1 tsp garlic powder
- 1/2 tsp dried dill
- 2 tbsp dried parsley
- 1/2 tsp pepper

Directions

1. Insert wire rack in rack position 8. Select slow cook, Set LOW for 6 hours. Press start to preheat the oven.
2. Spray dutch oven from inside with cooking spray.
3. Place pork chops into the dutch oven.
4. In a bowl, mix together the remaining ingredients and pour over pork chops.
5. Cover the dutch oven with lid and cook on low for 6 hours.
6. Serve and enjoy.

Nutritional Value (Amount per Serving):
- Calories 398
- Fat 26.6 g
- Carbohydrates 15.6 g
- Sugar 5.3 g
- Protein 23.1 g
- Cholesterol 82 mg

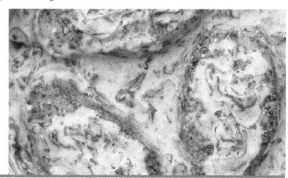

Slow Cooked Balsamic Pork Tenderloin

Prep Time	Cook Time	Serving
10 Minutes	6 hours	6

Ingredients

- 2 lbs pork tenderloin
- 1 tbsp cornstarch
- 1/2 cup brown sugar
- 1 garlic clove, crushed
- 1/4 tsp pepper
- 1/2 cup water
- 2 tbsp soy sauce
- 1/2 cup water
- 1/4 cup balsamic vinegar
- 1 tsp ground sage
- 1/2 tsp salt

Directions

1. Insert wire rack in rack position 8. Select slow cook, Set LOW for 6 hours. Press start to preheat the oven.
2. In a small bowl, mix together sage, garlic, pepper, and salt and rub over pork tenderloin.
3. Pour 1/2 cup water in the dutch oven and then place pork tenderloin in the dutch oven.
4. Cover with lid and cook on low for 6 hours.
5. For the glaze: in a saucepan, add brown sugar, soy sauce, water, vinegar, and cornstarch and heat over medium heat until thickens, about 4 minutes.
6. Brush glaze on pork during the last hour of cooking.
7. Serve and enjoy.

Nutritional Value (Amount per Serving):
- Calories 273
- Fat 5.3 g
- Carbohydrates 13.9 g
- Sugar 11.9 g
- Protein 40 g
- Cholesterol 110 mg

Chapter 5 Snack & Appetizer

BBQ Chickpeas

Prep Time	Cook Time	Serving
10 Minutes	12 Minutes	4

Ingredients

- 14 oz can chickpeas, rinsed, drained and pat dry
- 1 tbsp olive oil
- 1/2 tsp dry mustard
- 1/2 tsp garlic powder
- 1 tsp brown sugar
- 1 1/2 tsp paprika
- 1/4 tsp pepper
- 1/2 tsp celery salt

Directions

1. Insert wire rack in rack position 4. Select air fry, set temperature 375 F, timer for 12 minutes. Press start to preheat the oven.
2. Add chickpeas into the mixing bowl and toss with remaining ingredients.
3. Spread chickpeas on air fryer basket and air fry for 12 minutes.
4. Serve and enjoy.

Nutritional Value (Amount per Serving):
- Calories 154
- Fat 4.7 g
- Carbohydrates 24.1 g
- Sugar 0.6 g
- Protein 5.1 g
- Cholesterol 0 mg

Asian Tofu

Prep Time	Cook Time	Serving
10 Minutes	20 Minutes	4

Ingredients

- 1 block firm tofu, cut into 1-inch cubes
- 1 tsp vinegar
- 2 tbsp soy sauce
- 1 tbsp cornstarch
- 2 tsp sesame oil

Directions

1. Insert wire rack in rack position 4. Select air fry, set temperature 370 F, timer for 20 minutes. Press start to preheat the oven.
2. Add tofu, sesame oil, vinegar, and soy sauce in a large bowl and let marinate for 15 minutes.
3. Toss marinated tofu with cornstarch and place in the air fryer basket and air fry for 20 minutes.
4. Serve and enjoy.

Nutritional Value (Amount per Serving):
- Calories 48
- Fat 3.2 g
- Carbohydrates 2.8 g
- Sugar 0.3 g
- Protein 2.4 g
- Cholesterol 0 mg

Sweet Potato Fries

Prep Time	Cook Time	Serving
10 Minutes	8 Minutes	4

Ingredients

- 2 medium sweet potatoes, peeled and cut into fries shape
- 1/2 tsp garlic powder
- 1 tbsp olive oil
- 1/4 tsp chili powder
- 1/4 tsp cumin
- Pepper
- Salt

Directions

1. Insert wire rack in rack position 4. Select air fry, set temperature 400 F, timer for 8 minutes. Press start to preheat the oven.
2. Add sweet potato fries in a large bowl and drizzle with olive oil.
3. Sprinkle with chili powder, cumin, garlic powder, pepper, and salt and toss until well coated.
4. Transfer sweet potato fries in the air fryer basket and air fry for 8 minutes.
5. Serve and enjoy.

Nutritional Value (Amount per Serving):
- Calories 78
- Fat 2.4 g
- Carbohydrates 13.5 g
- Sugar 2.8 g
- Protein 1.1 g
- Cholesterol 0 mg

Chicken Tenders

Prep Time	Cook Time	Serving
10 Minutes	6 Minutes	8

Ingredients

- 1 egg
- 3 tbsp butter, melted
- 1/2 cup parmesan cheese, grated
- 8 piece chicken tenders
- 1 tsp Italian herbs
- 1 tsp garlic powder
- 1 cup breadcrumbs

Directions

1. Insert wire rack in rack position 4. Select air fry, set temperature 400 F, timer for 15 minutes. Press start to preheat the oven.
2. In a bowl, combine together egg, Italian herbs, garlic powder, and butter.
3. Add chicken tenders in the egg mixture and coat well.
4. In a shallow dish, combine together parmesan cheese and breadcrumbs.
5. Coat chicken with cheese and breadcrumbs mixture and set aside for 5 minutes.
6. Place coated chicken tenders in the air fryer basket and air fry for 6 minutes.
7. Serve and enjoy.

Nutritional Value (Amount per Serving):
- Calories 398
- Fat 17.6 g
- Carbohydrates 13.2 g
- Sugar 1 g
- Protein 46.3 g
- Cholesterol 161 mg

Jicama Fries

Prep Time	Cook Time	Serving
10 Minutes	20 Minutes	8

Ingredients

- 2 eggs, lightly beaten
- 1 tsp sea salt
- 1/2 large jicama, cut into fries
- 1 tbsp thyme, dried
- 3/4 cup arrowroot flour

Directions

1. Insert wire rack in rack position 4. Select air fry, set temperature 400 F, timer for 15 minutes. Press start to preheat the oven.
2. Add beaten eggs into the bowl.
3. Take one more bowl and combine together salt, thyme, and arrowroot flour.
4. Add jicama fries in eggs bowl and toss well.
5. Add jicama fries in flour mixture and toss until well coated.
6. Place coated jicama fries in the air fryer basket and air fry for 20 minutes.
7. Serve and enjoy.

Nutritional Value (Amount per Serving):
- Calories 52
- Fat 1.2 g
- Carbohydrates 8.4 g
- Sugar 1.4 g
- Protein 2.4 g
- Cholesterol 41 mg

Onion Rings

Prep Time	Cook Time	Serving
10 Minutes	8 Minutes	2

Ingredients

- 1 large egg, lightly beaten
- 1 medium onion, sliced into whole slices
- 1/2 cup breadcrumbs
- Pepper
- Salt

Directions

1. Insert wire rack in rack position 4. Select air fry, set temperature 350 F, timer for 8 minutes. Press start to preheat the oven.
2. Add breadcrumbs, pepper, and salt in a shallow dish.
3. In another shallow dish add lightly beaten egg.
4. Dip onion ring in egg then coats with breadcrumbs.
5. Place coated onion rings in the air fryer basket and air fry for 8 minutes.
6. Serve and enjoy.

Nutritional Value (Amount per Serving):
- Calories 165
- Fat 4 g
- Carbohydrates 24.8 g
- Sugar 4.2 g
- Protein 7.4 g
- Cholesterol 93 mg

Kale Chips

Prep Time	Cook Time	Serving
10 Minutes	3 Minutes	2

Ingredients

- 1 head kale, tear into 1 1/2 inch pieces
- 1 tsp soy sauce
- 1 tbsp olive oil

Directions

1. Insert wire rack in rack position 4. Select air fry, set temperature 400 F, timer for 3 minutes. Press start to preheat the oven.
2. Add kale in a bowl and toss with soy sauce and oil.
3. Add kale on the air fryer basket and air fry for 3 minutes.
4. Serve and enjoy.

Nutritional Value (Amount per Serving):
- Calories 78
- Fat 7 g
- Carbohydrates 3.7 g
- Sugar 0.1 g
- Protein 1.2 g
- Cholesterol 0 mg

Cod Sticks

Prep Time	Cook Time	Serving
10 Minutes	12 Minutes	4

Ingredients

- 1 lb cod
- 2 large eggs
- 1/2 tsp pepper
- 3 tbsp milk
- 1 cup almond flour
- 2 cups breadcrumbs
- 1/4 tsp sea salt

Directions

1. Insert wire rack in rack position 4. Select air fry, set temperature 350 F, timer for 12 minutes. Press start to preheat the oven.
2. In a small bowl, whisk together milk and eggs.
3. In a shallow dish, mix together breadcrumbs, pepper, and salt.
4. In another shallow dish, add the almond flour.
5. Roll cod sticks into the almond flour then dip in the egg mixture and finally coat with breadcrumbs.
6. Place coated cod sticks in the air fryer basket and air fry for 12 minutes.
7. Serve and enjoy.

Nutritional Value (Amount per Serving):
- Calories 543
- Fat 19.9 g
- Carbohydrates 45.8 g
- Sugar 4.1 g
- Protein 42.7 g
- Cholesterol 156 mg

Chicken Tikka

Prep Time	Cook Time	Serving
10 Minutes	15 Minutes	4

Ingredients

- 1 lb boneless chicken, cut into pieces
- 1 cup cherry tomatoes
- 1 tsp turmeric powder
- 2 tbsp coriander powder
- 2 tbsp cumin powder
- 2 tsp olive oil
- 1 cup yogurt
- 1 tbsp ginger garlic paste
- 2 tbsp red chili powder
- 3 bell peppers, cut into chunks
- Salt

Directions

1. Insert wire rack in rack position 4. Select air fry, set temperature 400 F, timer for 15 minutes. Press start to preheat the oven.
2. Add all ingredients into the mixing bowl and place it in the refrigerator for 2 hours.
3. Threading marinated chicken, pepper, and tomatoes alternately on soaked wooden skewers.
4. Place chicken skewers on air fryer basket and air fry for 15 minutes.
5. Serve and enjoy.

Nutritional Value (Amount per Serving):
- Calories 343
- Fat 13.2 g
- Carbohydrates 17.1 g
- Sugar 10.4 g
- Protein 38.7 g
- Cholesterol 105 mg

Baked Okra

Prep Time	Cook Time	Serving
10 Minutes	15 Minutes	4

Ingredients

- 1 lb fresh okra, cut into 3/4-inch pieces
- 1 tsp paprika
- 1/4 tsp chili powder
- 2 tbsp olive oil
- Salt

Directions

1. Line roasting pan with parchment paper and set aside.
2. Insert wire rack in rack position 6. Select bake, set temperature 390 F, timer for 15 minutes. Press start to preheat the oven.
3. Add okra, chili powder, paprika, oil, and salt into the bowl and toss well.
4. Spread okra on a roasting pan and bake for 15 minutes.
5. Serve and enjoy.

Nutritional Value (Amount per Serving):
- Calories 107
- Fat 7.3 g
- Carbohydrates 8.8 g
- Sugar 1.7 g
- Protein 2.3 g
- Cholesterol 0 mg

Salmon Croquettes

Prep Time	Cook Time	Serving
10 Minutes	7 Minutes	4

Ingredients

- 1 lb can red salmon, drained and mashed
- 2 eggs, beaten
- 1/3 cup olive oil
- 1 cup breadcrumbs

Directions

1. Insert wire rack in rack position 4. Select air fry, set temperature 400 F, timer for 7 minutes. Press start to preheat the oven.
2. In a bowl, add drained salmon, eggs, and parsley. Mix well.
3. In a shallow dish, combine together breadcrumbs and oil.
4. Make 16 croquettes from the salmon mixture and coat with breadcrumbs.
5. Place coated croquettes in the air fryer basket and air fry for 7 minutes.
6. Serve and enjoy.

Nutritional Value (Amount per Serving):
- Calories 330
- Fat 22.6 g
- Carbohydrates 19.6 g
- Sugar 1.8 g
- Protein 13.3 g
- Cholesterol 95 mg

Crispy Broccoli Florets

Prep Time	Cook Time	Serving
10 Minutes	10 Minutes	3

Ingredients

- 1 lb broccoli florets
- 2 tbsp plain yogurt
- 1 tbsp chickpea flour
- 1/2 tsp red chili powder
- 1/4 tsp turmeric powder
- 1/2 tsp salt

Directions

1. Insert wire rack in rack position 4. Select air fry, set temperature 400 F, timer for 10 minutes. Press start to preheat the oven.
2. Add all ingredients to the bowl and toss well.
3. Place marinated broccoli in a refrigerator for 15 minutes.
4. Place marinated broccoli into the air fryer basket and air fry for 10 minutes.
5. Serve and enjoy.

Nutritional Value (Amount per Serving):
- Calories 76
- Fat 1 g
- Carbohydrates 13.7 g
- Sugar 3.8 g
- Protein 5.7 g
- Cholesterol 1 mg

Eggplant Fries

Prep Time	Cook Time	Serving
10 Minutes	20 Minutes	4

Ingredients

- 1 eggplant, cut into 3-inch pieces
- 1 tbsp olive oil
- 4 tbsp cornstarch
- 2 tbsp water
- Salt

Directions

1. Insert wire rack in rack position 4. Select air fry, set temperature 390 F, timer for 20 minutes. Press start to preheat the oven.
2. In a bowl, mix together water, oil, eggplant, and cornstarch.
3. Place eggplant fries in the air fryer basket and air fry for 20 minutes.
4. Serve and enjoy.

Nutritional Value (Amount per Serving):
- Calories 89
- Fat 3.7 g
- Carbohydrates 14 g
- Sugar 3.4 g
- Protein 1.1 g
- Cholesterol 0 mg

Fish Nuggets

Prep Time	Cook Time	Serving
10 Minutes	20 Minutes	4

Ingredients

- 1 lb cod fillet, cut into nuggets
- 1 cup almond flour
- 1 cup breadcrumbs
- 4 tbsp olive oil
- 3 eggs, beaten
- 1 tsp salt

Directions

1. Insert wire rack in rack position 4. Select air fry, set temperature 490 F, timer for 20 minutes. Press start to preheat the oven.
2. Add beaten eggs in a bowl.
3. Add almond flour in a shallow dish.
4. In another bowl, combine together breadcrumbs, salt, and oil.
5. Coat fish pieces with flour then dip in eggs and finally coat with breadcrumbs.
6. Place coated fish nuggets in the air fryer basket and air fry for 20 minutes.
7. Serve and enjoy.

Nutritional Value (Amount per Serving):
- Calories 533
- Fat 33 g
- Carbohydrates 25.7 g
- Sugar 1.9 g
- Protein 34 g
- Cholesterol 178 mg

Herb Chicken Wings

Prep Time	Cook Time	Serving
10 Minutes	15 Minutes	6

Ingredients

- 4 lb chicken wings
- 1/4 tsp cinnamon
- 1 habanero, chopped
- 6 garlic cloves, minced
- 2 tbsp soy sauce
- 1 tbsp olive oil
- 4 tbsp vinegar
- 1 fresh lime juice
- 1/2 tbsp ginger, minced
- 1 tbsp brown sugar
- 1 tsp thyme, chopped
- 1/2 tsp white pepper
- 1/2 tsp salt

Directions

1. Insert wire rack in rack position 4. Select air fry, set temperature 390 F, timer for 15 minutes. Press start to preheat the oven.
2. Add all ingredients into the mixing bowl and mix well.
3. Place marinated chicken wings in a refrigerator for 2 hours.
4. Add chicken wings into the air fryer basket and air fry for 15 minutes.
5. Serve and enjoy.

Nutritional Value (Amount per Serving):
- Calories 617
- Fat 24.8 g
- Carbohydrates 4.9 g
- Sugar 2.2 g
- Protein 88.3 g
- Cholesterol 269 mg

Crab Croquettes

Prep Time	Cook Time	Serving
10 Minutes	18 Minutes	6

Ingredients

- 1 lb crab meat
- 2 egg whites
- 1/2 tsp parsley
- 1/4 tsp chives
- 1/4 tsp tarragon
- 2 tbsp celery, chopped
- 1/4 cup red pepper, chopped
- 1 cup breadcrumbs
- 1 tsp olive oil
- 1/2 tsp fresh lime juice
- 4 tbsp sour cream
- 4 tbsp mayonnaise
- 1/4 cup onion, chopped
- 1/4 tsp salt

Directions

1. Insert wire rack in rack position 4. Select air fry, set temperature 400 F, timer for 18 minutes. Press start to preheat the oven.
2. Place breadcrumbs and salt in a shallow dish.
3. In a small bowl, add egg whites.
4. Add all remaining ingredients into the mixing bowl and mix well.
5. Make small croquettes from the mixture and dip in egg white and coat with breadcrumbs.
6. Place croquettes in air fryer basket and air fry for 18 minutes.
7. Serve and enjoy.

Nutritional Value (Amount per Serving):
- Calories 211
- Fat 8.1 g
- Carbohydrates 18.3 g
- Sugar 2.4 g
- Protein 13.5 g
- Cholesterol 47 mg

Roasted Cashew

Prep Time	Cook Time	Serving
10 Minutes	10 Minutes	4

Ingredients

- 1 2/3 cups cashews
- 1 tsp olive oil
- 1 tsp red chili powder
- 1 tsp coriander powder
- 1/2 tsp black pepper
- 1/2 tsp salt

Directions

1. Insert wire rack in rack position 4. Select air fry, set temperature 250 F, timer for 10 minutes. Press start to preheat the oven.
2. Add all ingredients into the mixing bowl and toss well.
3. Add cashews in the air fryer basket and air fry for 10 minutes.
4. Serve or store.

Nutritional Value (Amount per Serving):
- Calories 340
- Fat 27.8 g
- Carbohydrates 19.2 g
- Sugar 2.9 g
- Protein 8.9 g
- Cholesterol 0 mg

Salmon Patties

Prep Time	Cook Time	Serving
10 Minutes	15 Minutes	4

Ingredients

- 1 egg
- 4 tbsp cup cornmeal
- 4 tbsp onion, minced
- 1/2 tsp garlic powder
- 2 tbsp mayonnaise
- 14 oz can salmon, drained
- 4 tbsp flour
- Pepper
- Salt

Directions

1. Insert wire rack in rack position 4. Select air fry, set temperature 350 F, timer for 15 minutes. Press start to preheat the oven.
2. Add drained salmon in a bowl and using a fork to make salmon flake.
3. Add garlic powder, mayonnaise, flour, cornmeal, egg, onion, pepper, and salt in a bowl. Mix well.
4. Make patties from mixture and place in air fryer basket and air fry for 15 minutes.
5. Serve and enjoy.

Nutritional Value (Amount per Serving):
- Calories 255
- Fat 10.9 g
- Carbohydrates 11.6 g
- Sugar 1.2 g
- Protein 26.2 g
- Cholesterol 86 mg

Roasted Mix Nuts

Prep Time	Cook Time	Serving
10 Minutes	5 Minutes	4

Ingredients

- 2 cup mix nuts
- 1 tsp ground cumin
- 1 tsp chipotle chili powder
- 1 tbsp butter, melted
- 1 tsp pepper
- 1 tsp salt

Directions

1. Insert wire rack in rack position 4. Select air fry, set temperature 350 F, timer for 5 minutes. Press start to preheat the oven.
2. In a mixing bowl, toss together all ingredients and until well mixed.
3. Add mix nuts in the air fryer basket and roast for 5 minutes.
4. Serve and enjoy.

Nutritional Value (Amount per Serving):

- Calories 473
- Fat 43.5 g
- Carbohydrates 16.8 g
- Sugar 3.3 g
- Protein 11.4 g
- Cholesterol 8 mg

Tasty Fishcakes

Prep Time	Cook Time	Serving
10 Minutes	15 Minutes	2

Ingredients

- 1 1/2 cups white fish, cooked
- 1 tbsp butter
- 1/2 cup mashed potatoes
- 1 1/2 tbsp milk
- 1/2 tsp sage
- 1 tsp parsley
- 2 tsp flour
- Pepper
- Salt

Directions

1. Insert wire rack in rack position 4. Select air fry, set temperature 400 F, timer for 15 minutes. Press start to preheat the oven.
2. Add all ingredients in a bowl and mix well.
3. Make patties from mixture and place in the refrigerator for 1 hour.
4. Place patties in the air fryer basket and air fry for 15 minutes.
5. Serve and enjoy.

Nutritional Value (Amount per Serving):

- Calories 206
- Fat 15 g
- Carbohydrates 12.5 g
- Sugar 0.5 g
- Protein 5.9 g
- Cholesterol 17 mg

Roasted Almond, Peanuts & Cashew

Prep Time	Cook Time	Serving
10 Minutes	15 Minutes	6

Ingredients

- 1/2 cup cashew nuts
- 1 cup peanuts
- 1 cup almonds
- 1 tbsp olive oil
- 1/2 tsp salt

Directions

1. Insert wire rack in rack position 4. Select air fry, set temperature 320 F, timer for 5 minutes. Press start to preheat the oven.
2. Add nuts in the air fryer basket and air fry for 10 minutes.
3. Transfer nuts into the bowl and toss with oil and salt.
4. Add nuts again in the air fryer basket and air fry for 5 minutes more.
5. Serve and enjoy.

Nutritional Value (Amount per Serving):
- Calories 315
- Fat 27.5 g
- Carbohydrates 11 g
- Sugar 2.2 g
- Protein 11.4 g
- Cholesterol 0 mg

Sweet Potato Fries

Prep Time	Cook Time	Serving
10 Minutes	15 Minutes	4

Ingredients

- 2 sweet potatoes, peel and cut into fries shape
- 1 tbsp olive oil
- 1/4 tsp garlic powder
- 1/4 tsp pepper
- 1/4 tsp salt

Directions

1. Insert wire rack in rack position 4. Select air fry, set temperature 400 F, timer for 15 minutes. Press start to preheat the oven.
2. Toss sweet potato fries in a bowl with oil, garlic powder, pepper, and salt.
3. Place sweet potatoes fries in the air fryer basket and cook for 15 minutes.
4. Serve and enjoy.

Nutritional Value (Amount per Serving):
- Calories 87
- Fat 3.5 g
- Carbohydrates 13.3 g
- Sugar 2.8 g
- Protein 1.1 g
- Cholesterol 0 mg

Healthy Carrots Chips

Prep Time	Cook Time	Serving
10 Minutes	15 Minutes	4

Ingredients

- 12 oz carrot chips
- 1/2 tsp garlic powder
- 1 tbsp olive oil
- 1/4 tsp paprika
- 1/4 tsp pepper
- 1/2 tsp salt

Directions

1. Insert wire rack in rack position 4. Select air fry, set temperature 375 F, timer for 12 minutes. Press start to preheat the oven.
2. Add all ingredients into the bowl and toss well.
3. Spray air fryer basket with cooking spray.
4. Transfer carrot chips to the air fryer basket and air fry for 15 minutes.
5. Serve and enjoy.

Nutritional Value (Amount per Serving):

- Calories 67
- Fat 3.5 g
- Carbohydrates 8.4 g
- Sugar 5.1 g
- Protein 1.1 g
- Cholesterol 0 mg

Sweet Pepper Poppers

Prep Time	Cook Time	Serving
10 Minutes	15 Minutes	10

Ingredients

- 1 lb mini sweet peppers, halved
- 1/2 cup feta cheese, crumbled
- 8 oz cream cheese
- 8 oz gouda cheese, grated
- 2 tbsp cilantro, chopped
- 2 garlic cloves, minced
- 1/4 cup onion, grated

Directions

1. Insert wire rack in rack position 4. Select air fry, set temperature 425 F, timer for 15 minutes. Press start to preheat the oven.
2. Add all ingredients except peppers into the bowl and mix well to combine.
3. Stuff each pepper halves with cheese mixture and place on an air fryer basket and air fry for 15 minutes.
4. Serve and enjoy.

Nutritional Value (Amount per Serving):

- Calories 186
- Fat 15.8 g
- Carbohydrates 2.8 g
- Protein 8.6 g
- Sugar 1.6 g
- Cholesterol 57mg

Potato Chips

Prep Time	Cook Time	Serving
10 Minutes	30 Minutes	2

Ingredients

- 1 medium potato, thinly sliced
- 1/8 tsp pepper
- 1/2 tsp oregano
- 1/4 tsp chili powder
- 2 tsp olive oil
- 1/8 tsp thyme
- 1/8 tsp rosemary
- Salt

Directions

1. Insert wire rack in rack position 4. Select air fry, set temperature 400 F, timer for 30 minutes. Press start to preheat the oven.
2. Add potato slices in a bowl.
3. Add remaining ingredients and toss well.
4. Arrange potato slices in the air fryer basket and air fry for 30 minutes.
5. Serve and enjoy.

Nutritional Value (Amount per Serving):
- Calories 124
- Fat 4.8 g
- Carbohydrates 19 g
- Sugar 0.9 g
- Protein 2.2 g
- Cholesterol 0 mg

Buffalo Baby Potatoes

Prep Time	Cook Time	Serving
10 Minutes	20 Minutes	4

Ingredients

- 1 lb baby potatoes
- 2 tbsp olive oil
- 1/4 cup buffalo sauce
- Pepper
- Salt

Directions

1. Insert wire rack in rack position 4. Select air fry, set temperature 375 F, timer for 20 minutes. Press start to preheat the oven.
2. Add baby potatoes in a large bowl with remaining ingredients and toss well.
3. Transfer potatoes in the air fryer basket and air fry for 20 minutes.
4. Serve and enjoy.

Nutritional Value (Amount per Serving):
- Calories 131
- Fat 7.6 g
- Carbohydrates 14.4 g
- Sugar 0.1 g
- Protein 2.9 g
- Cholesterol 0 mg

Cajun Potato Wedges

Prep Time	Cook Time	Serving
10 Minutes	25 Minutes	4

Ingredients

- 4 potatoes, cut into wedges
- 1 tbsp Cajun spice
- 1 tbsp olive oil
- Pepper
- Salt

Directions

1. Insert wire rack in rack position 4. Select air fry, set temperature 375 F, timer for 25 minutes. Press start to preheat the oven.
2. Add potato wedges in the air fryer basket and drizzle with olive oil and air fry for 25 minutes.
3. Transfer potato wedges in a mixing bowl and season with Cajun spice, pepper, and salt. Toss well.
4. Serve and enjoy.

Nutritional Value (Amount per Serving):
- Calories 177
- Fat 3 g
- Carbohydrates 33 g
- Sugar 2 g
- Protein 3 g
- Cholesterol 0 mg

Garlic Chili Okra

Prep Time	Cook Time	Serving
10 Minutes	12 Minutes	2

Ingredients

- 1/2 lb okra, trimmed and sliced
- 1 tsp olive oil
- 1/2 tsp chili powder
- 1/2 tsp garlic powder
- 1/8 tsp pepper
- 1/4 tsp salt

Directions

1. Insert wire rack in rack position 4. Select air fry, set temperature 350 F, timer for 12 minutes. Press start to preheat the oven.
2. Add all ingredients into the bowl and toss well.
3. Transfer okra into the air fryer basket and air fry for 12 minutes.
4. Serve and enjoy.

Nutritional Value (Amount per Serving):
- Calories 68
- Fat 2.6 g
- Carbohydrates 9 g
- Sugar 1.8 g
- Protein 2.3 g
- Cholesterol 0 mg

Crispy Chicken Wings

Prep Time	Cook Time	Serving
10 Minutes	15 Minutes	2

Ingredients

- 1 lb chicken wings
- 1/2 tsp smoked paprika
- 1/2 tsp herb de Provence
- Pepper
- Salt

Directions

1. Insert wire rack in rack position 4. Select air fry, set temperature 350 F, timer for 15 minutes. Press start to preheat the oven.
2. Season chicken wings with herb de Provence, paprika, pepper, and salt.
3. Place seasoned chicken wings in the air fryer basket and air fry for 15 minutes.
4. Serve and enjoy.

Nutritional Value (Amount per Serving):
- Calories 433
- Fat 16.9 g
- Carbohydrates 0.3 g
- Sugar 0.1 g
- Protein 65.7 g
- Cholesterol 202 mg

Tangy Chicken Tenders

Prep Time	Cook Time	Serving
10 Minutes	18 Minutes	4

Ingredients

- 1 lb chicken tenders
- 1/2 tsp ginger, minced
- 3 garlic cloves, minced
- 2 tbsp sesame oil
- 5 tbsp pineapple juice
- 1/2 tsp pepper

Directions

1. Insert wire rack in rack position 4. Select air fry, set temperature 350 F, timer for 18 minutes. Press start to preheat the oven.
2. Add all ingredients except chicken in a mixing bowl and mix well.
3. Skewer chicken and place in a bowl and marinate for 2 hours.
4. Place marinated chicken in the air fryer basket and air fry for 18 minutes.
5. Serve and enjoy.

Nutritional Value (Amount per Serving):
- Calories 299
- Fat 15 g
- Carbohydrates 5 g
- Sugar 2 g
- Protein 33 g
- Cholesterol 101 mg

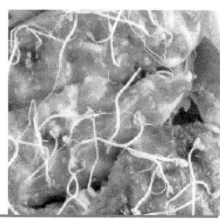

Air Fryer Apple Chips

Prep Time	Cook Time	Serving
10 Minutes	8 Minutes	4

Ingredients

- 1 large apple, sliced thinly
- 1/4 tsp ground cinnamon
- 1/4 tsp ground nutmeg

Directions

1. Insert wire rack in rack position 4. Select air fry, set temperature 375 F, timer for 8 minutes. Press start to preheat the oven.
2. Season apple slices with nutmeg and cinnamon.
3. Place apple slice in the air fryer basket and air fry for 8 minutes.
4. Serve and enjoy.

Nutritional Value (Amount per Serving):

- Calories 30
- Fat 0.2 g
- Carbohydrates 7.9 g
- Sugar 5.8 g
- Protein 0.2 g
- Cholesterol 0 mg

Chapter 6 Fish & Seafood

Lemon Walnut Salmon

Prep Time	Cook Time	Serving
10 Minutes	15 Minutes	4

Ingredients

- 4 salmon fillets
- 1/4 cup parmesan cheese, grated
- 1/4 cup walnuts
- 1 tsp olive oil
- 1 tbsp lemon rind

Directions

1. Spray a baking tray with cooking spray and set aside.
2. Insert wire rack in rack position 6. Select bake, set temperature 390 F, timer for 15 minutes. Press start to preheat the oven.
3. Place salmon fillets in the baking dish.
4. Add walnuts into the food processor and process until ground.
5. Mix together walnuts, cheese, oil, and lemon rind and spread on top of salmon fillets.
6. Bake for 15 minutes.
7. Serve and enjoy.

Nutritional Value (Amount per Serving):
- Calories 313
- Fat 18 g
- Carbohydrates 1.3 g
- Sugar 0.2 g
- Protein 38.3 g
- Cholesterol 83 mg

Flavorful Pesto Salmon

Prep Time	Cook Time	Serving
10 Minutes	20 Minutes	2

Ingredients

- 2 salmon fillets
- 1/4 cup parmesan cheese, grated

For pesto:
- 3 garlic cloves, peeled and chopped
- 1 1/2 cups fresh basil leaves
- 1/4 cup parmesan cheese, grated
- 1/4 cup pine nuts
- 1/4 cup olive oil
- 1/2 tsp pepper
- 1/2 tsp salt

Directions

1. Insert wire rack in rack position 6. Select bake, set temperature 390 F, timer for 20 minutes. Press start to preheat the oven.
2. Add all pesto ingredients into the blender and blend until smooth.
3. Place salmon fillet on a roasting pan. Spread 2 tablespoons of pesto on top of each salmon fillet. Sprinkle grated cheese on top.
4. Bake for 20 minutes.
5. Serve and enjoy.

Nutritional Value (Amount per Serving):
- Calories 614
- Fat 50.4 g
- Carbohydrates 4.9 g
- Sugar 0.7 g
- Protein 41.4 g
- Cholesterol 87 mg

Herb Baked Salmon

Prep Time	Cook Time	Serving
10 Minutes	30 Minutes	6

Ingredients

- 2 1/2 lbs large salmon fillet
- 2 cups cherry tomatoes, halved
- 1/2 cup olives pitted
- 2 lemons, sliced
- 1 tsp fresh thyme, chopped
- 1 tsp rosemary, chopped
- 1 tsp oregano, chopped
- 4 tbsp olive oil
- 1/4 cup onion, sliced
- 2 tsp capers
- Pepper
- Salt

Directions

1. Line roasting pan with parchment paper and set aside.
2. Insert wire rack in rack position 6. Select bake, set temperature 390 F, timer for 30 minutes. Press start to preheat the oven.
3. Place salmon fillets on a roasting pan.
4. Arrange lemon slices and olives, onions, capers, and tomatoes around the salmon. Drizzle with oil and season with pepper and salt.
5. Bake for 30 minutes.
6. Garnish with herbs and serve.

Nutritional Value (Amount per Serving):
- Calories 516
- Fat 36.9 g
- Carbohydrates 6.7 g
- Sugar 2.5 g
- Protein 3.2 g
- Cholesterol 0 mg

Cod with Potatoes & Tomatoes

Prep Time	Cook Time	Serving
10 Minutes	25 Minutes	4

Ingredients

- 1 lb cod fillet, cut into four pieces
- 4 tbsp olive oil
- 2 cups baby potatoes, diced
- 2 cups cherry tomatoes
- Pepper
- Salt

Directions

1. Insert wire rack in rack position 6. Select bake, set temperature 390 F, timer for 10 minutes. Press start to preheat the oven.
2. Toss potatoes with half olive oil and place in roasting pan. Bake potatoes for 15 minutes.
3. Remove roasting pan from oven and place cod fillets and cherry tomatoes in the pan.
4. Drizzle with remaining oil and season with pepper and salt.
5. Bake for 10 minutes.
6. Serve and enjoy.

Nutritional Value (Amount per Serving):
- Calories 238
- Fat 15.2 g
- Carbohydrates 5.9 g
- Sugar 2.4 g
- Protein 21.5 g
- Cholesterol 56 mg

Greek Salmon

Prep Time	Cook Time	Serving
10 Minutes	20 Minutes	4

Ingredients

- 4 salmon fillets
- 2 cups grape tomatoes, halved
- 1 onion, chopped
- 1/2 cup pesto
- 1/2 cup feta cheese, crumbled

Directions

1. Line roasting pan with parchment paper and set aside.
2. Insert wire rack in rack position 6. Select bake, set temperature 350 F, timer for 20 minutes. Press start to preheat the oven.
3. Place salmon fillet in roasting pan and top with tomatoes, onion, pesto, and cheese.
4. Bake for 20 minutes.
5. Serve and enjoy.

Nutritional Value (Amount per Serving):

- Calories 447
- Fat 28.2 g
- Carbohydrates 8.8 g
- Sugar 6.3 g
- Protein 41.3 g
- Cholesterol 103 mg

Cod with Vegetables

Prep Time	Cook Time	Serving
10 Minutes	22 Minutes	2

Ingredients

- 1 lb cod fish fillets
- 1/2 tsp oregano
- 1 leek, sliced
- 1 onion, quartered
- 2 tomatoes, halved
- 2 tbsp olive oil
- 1/2 tsp red pepper flakes
- 1/2 cup olives pitted and halved
- 8 asparagus spears
- Pepper
- Salt

Directions

1. Line roasting pan with parchment paper and set aside.
2. Insert wire rack in rack position 6. Select bake, set temperature 390 F, timer for 22 minutes. Press start to preheat the oven.
3. Arrange fish fillets, olives, tomatoes, onion, leek, and asparagus in roasting pan. Drizzle with olive oil and season with oregano, chili flakes, pepper, and salt.
4. Bake for 22 minutes.
5. Serve and enjoy.

Nutritional Value (Amount per Serving):

- Calories 487
- Fat 19.3 g
- Carbohydrates 22.3 g
- Sugar 9.2 g
- Protein 58.2 g
- Cholesterol 125 mg

Delicious Herb Sardines

Prep Time	Cook Time	Serving
10 Minutes	15 Minutes	4

Ingredients

- 1 lb sardines, rinsed and pat dry
- 1 1/2 tsp fresh parsley, chopped
- 1 tbsp fresh lime juice
- 1 1/2 tsp mustard
- 2 garlic cloves, minced
- 3 tbsp olive oil
- 1/2 tsp dry onion flakes
- 1/2 tsp paprika
- 1/2 tbsp oregano
- 1/4 tsp sea salt

Directions

1. Line roasting pan with parchment paper and set aside.
2. Insert wire rack in rack position 6. Select bake, set temperature 390 F, timer for 15 minutes. Press start to preheat the oven.
3. In a large bowl, mix all ingredients except sardines and parsley. Add sardines and coat well.
4. Place sardines in roasting pan and bake for 15 minutes or until cooked through.
5. Garnish with parsley and serve.

Nutritional Value (Amount per Serving):
- Calories 340
- Fat 24 g
- Carbohydrates 2.6 g
- Sugar 0.4 g
- Protein 28.5 g
- Cholesterol 161 mg

Italian Salmon

Prep Time	Cook Time	Serving
10 Minutes	30 Minutes	2

Ingredients

- 2 salmon filets
- 1/2 cup tomato, diced
- 1/2 cup olives, chopped
- 1 tbsp balsamic vinegar
- 1 tbsp parsley, chopped
- 1/3 cup feta cheese, crumbled
- 1 tbsp olive oil
- Pepper
- Salt

Directions

1. Line roasting pan with parchment paper and set aside.
2. Insert wire rack in rack position 6. Select bake, set temperature 350 F, timer for 15 minutes. Press start to preheat the oven.
3. Season salmon with pepper and salt.
4. Place salmon in roasting pan and bake for 15 minutes.
5. Meanwhile, mix together tomato, olive oil, vinegar, olives, feta cheese, and parsley.
6. Remove salmon from oven and top with tomato olive mixture.
7. Serve and enjoy.

Nutritional Value (Amount per Serving):
- Calories 607
- Fat 20 g
- Carbohydrates 24.1 g
- Sugar 2.3 g
- Protein 4.3 g
- Cholesterol 22 mg

Flavorful Lemon Fish Fillets

Prep Time	Cook Time	Serving
10 Minutes	18 Minutes	4

Ingredients

- 1 lb tilapia fillets
- 1/2 tsp dried oregano
- 1 tsp fresh lemon juice
- 2 tsp olive oil
- 1 lemon, sliced
- 1 tsp garlic powder
- 1/2 tsp dried thyme
- 1/2 tsp pepper
- 1 tsp salt

Directions

1. Line roasting pan with parchment paper and set aside.
2. Insert wire rack in rack position 6. Select bake, set temperature 390 F, timer for 18 minutes. Press start to preheat the oven.
3. Place a fish fillets in roasting pan and brush with lemon juice and olive oil.
4. Mix together garlic powder, thyme, oregano, pepper, and salt and sprinkle over fish fillets. Place lemon slices at the top of the fish fillet.
5. Bake for 15-18 minutes or until cooked through.
6. Serve and enjoy.

Nutritional Value (Amount per Serving):
- Calories 118
- Fat 3.4 g
- Carbohydrates 1.1 g
- Sugar 0.3 g
- Protein 21.3 g
- Cholesterol 55 mg

Fish Fillets with Zucchini

Prep Time	Cook Time	Serving
10 Minutes	20 Minutes	2

Ingredients

- 8 oz cod fillets
- 1 tbsp olive oil
- 1/2 cup olives
- 1/2 cup cherry tomatoes halved
- 1 bell pepper, sliced
- 1 tbsp balsamic vinegar
- 1 lemon, sliced
- 3 garlic cloves, minced
- Pepper
- Salt

Directions

1. Insert wire rack in rack position 6. Select bake, set temperature 390 F, timer for 20 minutes. Press start to preheat the oven.
2. Place all vegetables in a baking dish. Season with pepper and salt and drizzle with oil. Bake vegetables for 10 minutes.
3. Season fish fillets with pepper and salt and drizzle with oil.
4. Place fish fillets in the baking dish with cooked vegetables.
5. Arrange lemon slices on top of fish fillets. Drizzle fish fillets and veggies with vinegar.
6. Bake for 10 minutes.
7. Serve and enjoy.

Nutritional Value (Amount per Serving):
- Calories 223
- Fat 11.8 g
- Carbohydrates 9.5 g
- Sugar 3.7 g
- Protein 21.7 g
- Cholesterol 56 mg

Dijon Herb Salmon

Prep Time	Cook Time	Serving
10 Minutes	15 Minutes	4

Ingredients

- 4 salmon fillets
- 1 tsp dried thyme
- 2 tbsp fresh lemon juice
- 2 tbsp Dijon mustard
- 2 tomatoes, sliced
- 1 small onion, sliced
- 1 tsp dried oregano
- 1 tsp dried rosemary
- Pepper
- Salt

Directions

1. Spray a baking dish with cooking spray and set aside.
2. Insert wire rack in rack position 6. Select bake, set temperature 390 F, timer for 15 minutes. Press start to preheat the oven.
3. In a bowl, mix together lemon juice, oregano, rosemary, thyme, mustard, pepper, and salt.
4. Add fish fillets and coat well form both sides. Cover and place in the refrigerator for 30 minutes.
5. Arrange sliced tomatoes and onion in the baking dish then place marinated fish fillets on top. Pour remaining marinade over fish fillets.
6. Bake for 15 minutes.
7. Serve and enjoy.

Nutritional Value (Amount per Serving):
- Calories 264
- Fat 11.6 g
- Carbohydrates 5.2 g
- Sugar 2.6 g
- Protein 35.7 g
- Cholesterol 78 mg

Jalapeno Salmon

Prep Time	Cook Time	Serving
10 Minutes	30 Minutes	6

Ingredients

- 2 lbs salmon fillet, skinless
- 1 lemon, sliced
- 1 orange, sliced
- 1 fennel bulb, sliced
- 3/4 cup olive oil
- 4 dill sprigs
- 1 jalapeno pepper, sliced
- Pepper
- Salt

Directions

1. Insert wire rack in rack position 6. Select bake, set temperature 325 F, timer for 30 minutes. Press start to preheat the oven.
2. Mix dill, jalapeno, lemon slices, orange slices, fennel in baking dish.
3. Season salmon with pepper and salt and place on top of the dill mixture.
4. Pour oil over salmon and bake for 30 minutes.
5. Serve and enjoy.

Nutritional Value (Amount per Serving):
- Calories 449
- Fat 34.8 g
- Carbohydrates 7.9 g
- Sugar 3 g
- Protein 30.6 g
- Cholesterol 67 mg

Air Fryer Salmon

Prep Time	Cook Time	Serving
10 Minutes	8 Minutes	4

Ingredients

- 4 salmon fillets
- 1 tbsp honey
- 2 tsp soy sauce
- 1 tsp sesame seeds, toasted
- Pepper
- Salt

Directions

1. Insert wire rack in rack position 4. Select air fry, set temperature 375 F, timer for 8 minutes. Press start to preheat the oven.
2. Brush salmon with soy sauce and season with pepper and salt.
3. Place salmon on air fryer basket and air fry for 8 minutes.
4. Brush salmon with honey and sprinkle with sesame seeds.
5. Serve and enjoy.

Nutritional Value (Amount per Serving):

- Calories 257
- Fat 11.4 g
- Carbohydrates 4.7 g
- Sugar 4.4 g
- Protein 34.9 g
- Cholesterol 78 mg

Asian Salmon

Prep Time	Cook Time	Serving
10 Minutes	10 Minutes	2

Ingredients

- 2 salmon fillets, skinless and boneless
- For marinade:
- 2 tbsp scallions, minced
- 1 tbsp ginger, grated
- 2 garlic cloves, minced
- 2 tbsp mirin
- 2 tbsp soy sauce

Directions

1. Insert wire rack in rack position 4. Select air fry, set temperature 360 F, timer for 10 minutes. Press start to preheat the oven.
2. Add all marinade ingredients into the zip-lock bag and mix well.
3. Add salmon in a zip-lock bag. The sealed bag shakes well and places it in the refrigerator for 60 minutes.
4. Arrange marinated salmon fillets on the air fryer basket and the air fryer for 10 minutes.
5. Serve and enjoy.

Nutritional Value (Amount per Serving):

- Calories 345
- Fat 18.2 g
- Carbohydrates 11.6 g
- Sugar 4.5 g
- Protein 36.1 g
- Cholesterol 78 mg

Paprika Herb Salmon

Prep Time	Cook Time	Serving
10 Minutes	5 Minutes	2

Ingredients

- 2 salmon fillets
- 1/4 tsp paprika
- 1 tsp herb de Provence
- 1 tbsp butter, melted
- 2 tbsp olive oil
- Pepper
- Salt

Directions

1. Insert wire rack in rack position 4. Select air fry, set temperature 390 F, timer for 5 minutes. Press start to preheat the oven.
2. Brush fish fillets with olive oil and sprinkle with paprika, herb de Provence, pepper, and salt.
3. Place fish fillets on air fryer basket and air fry for 5 minutes.
4. Drizzle salmon with butter and serve.

Nutritional Value (Amount per Serving):

- Calories 415
- Fat 31.2 g
- Carbohydrates 0.2 g
- Sugar 0 g
- Protein 35.6 g
- Cholesterol 94 mg

Honey Chili Salmon

Prep Time	Cook Time	Serving
10 Minutes	12 Minutes	3

Ingredients

- 3 salmon fillets
- 1/2 tsp chili powder
- 1/2 tsp turmeric
- 1 tsp coriander
- 1/4 cup honey
- 1 tbsp red pepper flakes
- Pepper
- Salt

Directions

1. Insert wire rack in rack position 4. Select air fry, set temperature 400 F, timer for 12 minutes. Press start to preheat the oven.
2. Add honey in microwave-safe bowl and microwave until just warm. Add red pepper flakes, chili powder, turmeric, coriander, pepper, and salt in honey and stir well.
3. Brush salmon fillets with honey and place on an air fryer basket and air fry for 12 minutes.
4. Serve and enjoy.

Nutritional Value (Amount per Serving):

- Calories 330
- Fat 11.4 g
- Carbohydrates 24.8 g
- Sugar 23.4 g
- Protein 34.9 g
- Cholesterol 78 mg

Easy Salmon Patties

Prep Time	Cook Time	Serving
10 Minutes	7 Minutes	2

Ingredients

- 8 oz salmon fillet, minced
- 1/4 tsp garlic powder
- 1/4 tsp onion powder
- 1 egg, lightly beaten
- Pepper
- Salt

Directions

1. Insert wire rack in rack position 4. Select air fry, set temperature 390 F, timer for 7 minutes. Press start to preheat the oven.
2. Add all ingredients into the bowl and mix until well combined.
3. Make small patties from salmon mixture and place on an air fryer basket and air fry for 7 minutes.
4. Serve and enjoy.

Nutritional Value (Amount per Serving):
- Calories 184
- Fat 9.2 g
- Carbohydrates 0.7 g
- Sugar 0.4 g
- Protein 24.9 g
- Cholesterol 132 mg

Cajun Butter Salmon

Prep Time	Cook Time	Serving
10 Minutes	8 Minutes	4

Ingredients

- 4 salmon fillets
- 1 tsp Cajun seasoning
- 1/4 cup butter, melted
- Pepper
- Salt

Directions

1. Insert wire rack in rack position 4. Select air fry, set temperature 375 F, timer for 8 minutes. Press start to preheat the oven.
2. Brush salmon fillets with butter and season with Cajun seasoning, pepper, and salt.
3. Place salmon fillets on an air fryer basket and air fry for 8 minutes.
4. Serve and enjoy.

Nutritional Value (Amount per Serving):
- Calories 337
- Fat 22.5 g
- Carbohydrates 0 g
- Sugar 0 g
- Protein 34.7 g
- Cholesterol 109 mg

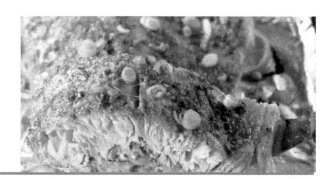

Tuna Patties

Prep Time	Cook Time	Serving
10 Minutes	10 Minutes	10

Ingredients

- 15 oz can tuna, drained and flaked
- 3 tbsp parmesan cheese, grated
- 1/2 cup breadcrumbs
- 1 tbsp lemon juice
- 2 eggs, lightly beaten
- 1/2 tsp dried herbs
- 1/2 tsp garlic powder
- 2 tbsp onion, minced
- 1 celery stalk, chopped
- Pepper
- Salt

Directions

1. Line air fryer basket with parchment paper and set aside.
2. Insert wire rack in rack position 4. Select air fry, set temperature 360 F, timer for 10 minutes. Press start to preheat the oven.
3. Add all ingredients into the mixing bowl and mix until well combined.
4. Make small patties from tuna mixture and place on an air fryer basket and air fry for 10 minutes.
5. Serve and enjoy.

Nutritional Value (Amount per Serving):
- Calories 91
- Fat 1.9 g
- Carbohydrates 4.4 g
- Sugar 0.6 g
- Protein 13.3 g
- Cholesterol 47 mg

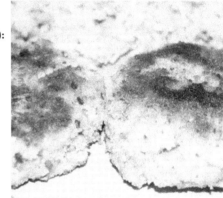

Lemon Pepper Fish Fillets

Prep Time	Cook Time	Serving
10 Minutes	10 Minutes	2

Ingredients

- 2 tilapia fillets
- 1/2 tsp lemon pepper seasoning
- 1/2 tsp garlic powder
- 1/2 tsp onion powder
- Salt

Directions

1. Line air fryer basket with parchment paper and set aside.
2. Insert wire rack in rack position 4. Select air fry, set temperature 360 F, timer for 10 minutes. Press start to preheat the oven.
3. Spray fish fillets with cooking spray and place in the air fryer basket. Season chicken with onion powder, lemon pepper seasoning, and salt.
4. Air fry fish fillets for 10 minutes.
5. Serve and enjoy.

Nutritional Value (Amount per Serving):
- Calories 99
- Fat 1.1 g
- Carbohydrates 1.3 g
- Sugar 0.4 g
- Protein 21.3 g
- Cholesterol 55 mg

Delicious Spicy Shrimp

Prep Time	Cook Time	Serving
10 Minutes	6 Minutes	4

Ingredients

- 1 lb shrimp
- 1/4 tsp red pepper flakes
- 2 garlic cloves, minced
- 2 tsp olive oil
- 1 tbsp parsley, chopped
- 2 tsp fresh lemon juice
- 1 tsp lemon zest, grated
- 1 tsp steak seasoning
- Pepper
- Salt

Directions

Directions:
1. Line air fryer basket with parchment paper and set aside.
2. Insert wire rack in rack position 4. Select air fry, set temperature 400 F, timer for 6 minutes. Press start to preheat the oven.
3. Add shrimp and remaining ingredients into the large bowl and toss well.
4. Spread shrimp on an air fryer basket and air fry for 6 minutes.
5. Serve and enjoy.

Nutritional Value (Amount per Serving):
- Calories 159
- Fat 4.3 g
- Carbohydrates 2.5 g
- Sugar 0.1 g
- Protein 26 g
- Cholesterol 239 mg

Easy Shrimp Casserole

Prep Time	Cook Time	Serving
10 Minutes	12 Minutes	4

Ingredients

- 1 lb shrimp, peeled and deveined
- 1/2 cup breadcrumbs
- 1/4 cup butter, melted
- 2 tbsp wine
- 1 tbsp garlic, minced
- 2 tbsp fresh parsley, chopped
- Pepper
- Salt

Directions

1. Spray a baking dish with cooking spray and set aside.
2. Insert wire rack in rack position 6. Select bake, set temperature 390 F, timer for 12 minutes. Press start to preheat the oven.
3. Add shrimp into the large bowl. Pour remaining ingredients over shrimp and toss well.
4. Pour shrimp mixture into the baking dish and bake for 12 minutes.
5. Serve and enjoy.

Nutritional Value (Amount per Serving):
- Calories 300
- Fat 14.2 g
- Carbohydrates 12.5 g
- Sugar 1 g
- Protein 28 g
- Cholesterol 269 mg

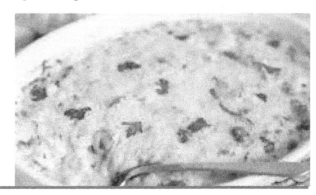

Chapter 7 Vegetables

Dehydrated Cucumber Chips

Prep Time	Cook Time	Serving
10 Minutes	12 hours	3

Ingredients

- 1 cucumber, sliced
- Pepper
- Salt

Directions

1. Arrange cucumber slices on the dehydrate basket in a single layer. Season with pepper and salt.
2. Insert wire rack in rack position 4. Select DEHYDRATE, set temperature 135 F, timer for 12 hours. Press start.
3. Dehydrate cucumber slices for 12 hours.

Nutritional Value (Amount per Serving):
- Calories 15
- Fat 0.1 g
- Carbohydrates 3.7 g
- Sugar 1.7 g
- Protein 0.7 g
- Cholesterol 0 mg

Dehydrated Broccoli Florets

Prep Time	Cook Time	Serving
10 Minutes	12 hours	6

Ingredients

- 1 lb broccoli florets
- Pepper
- Salt

Directions

1. Arrange broccoli florets on the dehydrate basket in a single layer. Season with pepper and salt.
2. Insert wire rack in rack position 4. Select DEHYDRATE, set temperature 115 F, timer for 12 hours. Press start.
3. Dehydrate broccoli florets for 12 hours.

Nutritional Value (Amount per Serving):
- Calories 26
- Fat 0.3 g
- Carbohydrates 5 g
- Sugar 1.3 g
- Protein 2.1 g
- Cholesterol 0 mg

Dehydrated Zucchini Chips

Prep Time	Cook Time	Serving
10 Minutes	6 hours	3

Ingredients

- 1 zucchini, sliced thinly
- 1/4 tsp garlic powder
- 1/4 tsp chili powder
- 1/8 tsp paprika
- Salt

Directions

1. Toss zucchini slices with garlic powder, chili powder, paprika, and salt.
2. Arrange zucchini slices on the dehydrate basket in a single layer.
3. Insert wire rack in rack position 4. Select DEHYDRATE, set temperature 135 F, timer for 6 hours. Press start.
4. Dehydrate zucchini slices for 6 hours.

Nutritional Value (Amount per Serving):
- Calories 12
- Fat 0.2 g
- Carbohydrates 2.5 g
- Sugar 1.2 g
- Protein 0.9 g
- Cholesterol 0 mg

Dehydrated Beet Slices

Prep Time	Cook Time	Serving
10 Minutes	10 hours	2

Ingredients

- 1 beet, sliced thinly
- Salt

Directions

1. Arrange beet slices on the dehydrate basket in a single layer. Season with salt.
2. Insert wire rack in rack position 4. Select DEHYDRATE, set temperature 135 F, timer for 10 hours. Press start.
3. Dehydrate beet slices for 10 hours.

Nutritional Value (Amount per Serving):
- Calories 22
- Fat 0.1 g
- Carbohydrates 5 g
- Sugar 4 g
- Protein 0.8 g
- Cholesterol 0 mg

Dehydrated Tomato Slices

Prep Time	Cook Time	Serving
10 Minutes	12 hours	4

Ingredients

- 4 tomatoes, sliced thinly
- Pepper
- Salt

Directions

1. Arrange tomato slices on the dehydrate basket in a single layer. Season with pepper and salt.
2. Insert wire rack in rack position 4. Select DEHYDRATE, set temperature 135 F, timer for 12 hours. Press start.
3. Dehydrate tomato slices for 12 hours.

Nutritional Value (Amount per Serving):
- Calories 22
- Fat 0.3 g
- Carbohydrates 4.8 g
- Sugar 3.2 g
- Protein 1.1 g
- Cholesterol 0 mg

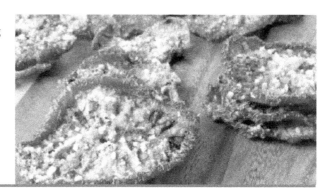

Dehydrated Green Beans

Prep Time	Cook Time	Serving
10 Minutes	12 hours	4

Ingredients

- 1 lb green beans
- Salt

Directions

1. Arrange green beans on the dehydrate basket in a single layer. Season with salt.
2. Insert wire rack in rack position 4. Select DEHYDRATE, set temperature 125 F, timer for 12 hours. Press start.
3. Dehydrate green beans for 12 hours.

Nutritional Value (Amount per Serving):
- Calories 35
- Fat 0.1 g
- Carbohydrates 8.1 g
- Sugar 1.6 g
- Protein 2.1 g
- Cholesterol 0 mg

Dehydrated Parsnips Slices

Prep Time	Cook Time	Serving
10 Minutes	10 hours	3

Ingredients

- 2 parsnips, peel & thinly sliced
- Salt

Directions

1. Arrange parsnips slices on the dehydrate basket in a single layer. Season with salt.
2. Insert wire rack in rack position 4. Select DEHYDRATE, set temperature 115 F, timer for 10 hours. Press start.
3. Dehydrate parsnips slices for 10 hours.

Nutritional Value (Amount per Serving):
- Calories 100
- Fat 0.4 g
- Carbohydrates 23.9 g
- Sugar 6.4 g
- Protein 1.6 g
- Cholesterol 0 mg

Dehydrated Carrot Slices

Prep Time	Cook Time	Serving
10 Minutes	10 hours	4

Ingredients

- 2 carrots, peel & thinly sliced
- Salt

Directions

1. Arrange carrot slices on the dehydrate basket in a single layer. Season with salt.
2. Insert wire rack in rack position 4. Select DEHYDRATE, set temperature 115 F, timer for 10 hours. Press start.
3. Dehydrate carrot slices for 10 hours.

Nutritional Value (Amount per Serving):
- Calories 13
- Fat 0 g
- Carbohydrates 3 g
- Sugar 1.5 g
- Protein 0.3 g
- Cholesterol 0 mg

Dehydrated Parsnips Slices

Prep Time	Cook Time	Serving
10 Minutes	10 hours	2

Ingredients

- 2 zucchini, thinly sliced
- 2 tbsp parmesan cheese, grated
- Salt

Directions

1. Arrange zucchini slices on the dehydrate basket in a single layer. Season with salt and sprinkle with cheese.
2. Insert wire rack in rack position 4. Select DEHYDRATE, set temperature 135 F, timer for 10 hours. Press start.
3. Dehydrate zucchini slices for 10 hours.

Nutritional Value (Amount per Serving):
- Calories 50
- Fat 1.6 g
- Carbohydrates 6.8 g
- Sugar 3.4 g
- Protein 4.2 g
- Cholesterol 4 mg

Dehydrated Dragon Fruit Slices

Prep Time	Cook Time	Serving
10 Minutes	12 hours	4

Ingredients

- 2 dragon fruit, peel & cut into 1/4-inch thick slices

Directions

1. Arrange dragon fruit slices on the dehydrate basket in a single layer.
2. Insert wire rack in rack position 4. Select DEHYDRATE, set temperature 115 F, timer for 12 hours. Press start.
3. Dehydrate dragon fruit slices for 12 hours.

Nutritional Value (Amount per Serving):
- Calories 23
- Fat 0 g
- Carbohydrates 6 g
- Sugar 6 g
- Protein 0 g
- Cholesterol 0 mg

Dehydrated Orange Slices

Prep Time	Cook Time	Serving
10 Minutes	12 hours	4

Ingredients

- 2 oranges, peel & cut into slices

Directions

1. Arrange orange slices on the dehydrate basket in a single layer.
2. Insert wire rack in rack position 4. Select DEHYDRATE, set temperature 135 F, timer for 12 hours. Press start.
3. Dehydrate orange slices for 12 hours.

Nutritional Value (Amount per Serving):
- Calories 43
- Fat 0.1 g
- Carbohydrates 10.8 g
- Sugar 8.6 g
- Protein 0.9 g
- Cholesterol 0 mg

Dehydrated Kiwi Slices

Prep Time	Cook Time	Serving
10 Minutes	12 hours	4

Ingredients

- 2 kiwis, peeled & cut into 1/4-inch thick slices

Directions

1. Arrange kiwi fruit slices on the dehydrate basket in a single layer.
2. Insert wire rack in rack position 4. Select DEHYDRATE, set temperature 135 F, timer for 12 hours. Press start.
3. Dehydrate kiwi slices for 12 hours.

Nutritional Value (Amount per Serving):
- Calories 23
- Fat 0.2 g
- Carbohydrates 5.6 g
- Sugar 3.4 g
- Protein 0.4 g
- Cholesterol 0 mg

Dehydrated Cinnamon Zucchini Slices

Prep Time	Cook Time	Serving
10 Minutes	12 hours	4

Ingredients

- 1 zucchini, sliced thinly
- 1 tsp ground cinnamon

Directions

1. Arrange zucchini slices on the dehydrate basket in a single layer. Sprinkle with cinnamon.
2. Insert wire rack in rack position 4. Select DEHYDRATE, set temperature 135 F, timer for 12 hours. Press start.
3. Dehydrate zucchini slices for 12 hours.

Nutritional Value (Amount per Serving):
- Calories 9
- Fat 0.1 g
- Carbohydrates 2.1 g
- Sugar 0.9 g
- Protein 0.6 g
- Cholesterol 0 mg

Dehydrated Cinnamon Apple Slices

Prep Time	Cook Time	Serving
10 Minutes	8 hours	4

Ingredients

- 2 apples, cut into 1/8-inch thick slices
- 1 tsp ground cinnamon

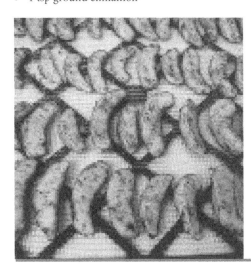

Directions

1. Arrange apple slices on the dehydrate basket in a single layer. Sprinkle cinnamon on apple slices.
2. Insert wire rack in rack position 4. Select DEHYDRATE, set temperature 135 F, timer for 8 hours. Press start.
3. Dehydrate apple slices for 8 hours.

Nutritional Value (Amount per Serving):
- Calories 59
- Fat 0.2 g
- Carbohydrates 15.9 g
- Sugar 11.6 g
- Protein 0.3 g
- Cholesterol 0 mg

Dehydrated Spicy Eggplant Slices

Prep Time	Cook Time	Serving
10 Minutes	6 hours	2

Ingredients

- 1 medium eggplant, cut into 1/4-inch thick slices
- 2 tsp paprika
- Salt

Directions

1. Arrange eggplant slices on the dehydrate basket in a single layer. Season with salt.
2. Insert wire rack in rack position 4. Select DEHYDRATE, set temperature 140 F, timer for 6 hours. Press start.
3. Dehydrate eggplant slices for 6 hours.

Nutritional Value (Amount per Serving):
- Calories 63
- Fat 0.7 g
- Carbohydrates 14.6 g
- Sugar 7.1 g
- Protein 2.6 g
- Cholesterol 0 mg

Dehydrated Banana Slices

Prep Time	Cook Time	Serving
10 Minutes	6 hours	2

Ingredients

- 2 bananas, peel & cut into 1/8-inch thick slices

Directions

1. Arrange banana slices on the dehydrate basket in a single layer.
2. Insert wire rack in rack position 4. Select DEHYDRATE, set temperature 135 F, timer for 6 hours. Press start.
3. Dehydrate banana slices for 6 hours.

Nutritional Value (Amount per Serving):
- Calories 105
- Fat 0.4 g
- Carbohydrates 27 g
- Sugar 14.4 g
- Protein 1.3 g
- Cholesterol 0 mg

Dehydrated Chickpeas

Prep Time	Cook Time	Serving
10 Minutes	10 hours	4

Ingredients

- 10 oz can chickpeas, drained and rinsed
- Salt

Directions

1. Arrange chickpeas on the dehydrate basket in a single layer. Season with salt.
2. Insert wire rack in rack position 4. Select DEHYDRATE, set temperature 135 F, timer for 10 hours. Press start.
3. Dehydrate chickpeas for 10 hours.

Nutritional Value (Amount per Serving):

- Calories 84
- Fat 0.8 g
- Carbohydrates 16 g
- Sugar 0 g
- Protein 3.5 g
- Cholesterol 0 mg

Dehydrated Pineapple Chunks

Prep Time	Cook Time	Serving
10 Minutes	12 hours	2

Ingredients

- 1 cup pineapple chunks

Directions

1. Arrange pineapple chunks on the dehydrate basket in a single layer.
2. Insert wire rack in rack position 4. Select DEHYDRATE, set temperature 135 F, timer for 12 hours. Press start.
3. Dehydrate pineapple chunks for 12 hours.

Nutritional Value (Amount per Serving):

- Calories 41
- Fat 0.1 g
- Carbohydrates 10.8 g
- Sugar 8.1 g
- Protein 0.4 g
- Cholesterol 0 mg

Dehydrated Summer Squash Chips

Prep Time	Cook Time	Serving
10 Minutes	10 hours	2

Ingredients

- 1 yellow summer squash, sliced thinly
- Pepper
- Salt

Directions

1. Arrange squash slices on the dehydrate basket in a single layer. Season with pepper & salt.
2. Insert wire rack in rack position 4. Select DEHYDRATE, set temperature 115 F, timer for 10 hours. Press start.
3. Dehydrate squash slices for 10 hours.

Nutritional Value (Amount per Serving):
- Calories 7
- Fat 0 g
- Carbohydrates 1.8 g
- Sugar 0.8 g
- Protein 0.3 g
- Cholesterol 0 mg

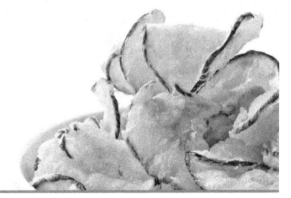

Dehydrated Okra

Prep Time	Cook Time	Serving
10 Minutes	25 hours	2

Ingredients

- 6 pods okra, slice into rounds

Directions

1. Arrange okra slices on the dehydrate basket in a single layer.
2. Insert wire rack in rack position 4. Select DEHYDRATE, set temperature 130 F, timer for 24 hours. Press start.
3. Dehydrate okra slices for 24 hours.

Nutritional Value (Amount per Serving):
- Calories 54
- Fat 0.6 g
- Carbohydrates 10.8 g
- Sugar 5.7 g
- Protein 4.5 g
- Cholesterol 0 mg

Dehydrated Lemon Slices

Prep Time	Cook Time	Serving
10 Minutes	10 hours	4

Ingredients

- 2 lemons, cut into 1/4-inch thick slices

Directions

1. Arrange lemon slices on the dehydrate basket in a single layer.
2. Insert wire rack in rack position 4. Select DEHYDRATE, set temperature 125 F, timer for 10 hours. Press start.
3. Dehydrate lemon slices for 10 hours.

Nutritional Value (Amount per Serving):
- Calories 8
- Fat 0.1 g
- Carbohydrates 2.7 g
- Sugar 0.7 g
- Protein 0.3 g
- Cholesterol 0 mg

Dehydrated Pear Slices

Prep Time	Cook Time	Serving
10 Minutes	5 hours	4

Ingredients

- 2 pears, cut into 1/4-inch thick slices

Directions

1. Arrange pear slices on the dehydrate basket in a single layer.
2. Insert wire rack in rack position 4. Select DEHYDRATE, set temperature 160 F, timer for 5 hours. Press start.
3. Dehydrate pear slices for 5 hours.

Nutritional Value (Amount per Serving):
- Calories 60
- Fat 0.2 g
- Carbohydrates 15.9 g
- Sugar 10.2 g
- Protein 0.4 g
- Cholesterol 0 mg

Dehydrated Mushroom Chips

Prep Time	Cook Time	Serving
10 Minutes	5 hours	4

Ingredients

- 1 cup mushrooms, clean and cut into 1/8-inch thick slices
- Salt

Directions

1. Arrange mushroom slices on the dehydrate basket in a single layer. Season with salt.
2. Insert wire rack in rack position 4. Select DEHYDRATE, set temperature 160 F, timer for 5 hours. Press start.
3. Dehydrate mushroom slices for 5 hours.

Nutritional Value (Amount per Serving):

- Calories 4
- Fat 0.1 g
- Carbohydrates 0.6 g
- Sugar 0.3 g
- Protein 0.6 g
- Cholesterol 0 mg

Dehydrated Snap Peas

Prep Time	Cook Time	Serving
10 Minutes	8 hours	4

Ingredients

- 2 cups snap peas
- Salt

Directions

1. Arrange snap peas on the dehydrate basket in a single layer. Season with salt.
2. Insert wire rack in rack position 4. Select DEHYDRATE, set temperature 135 F, timer for 8 hours. Press start.
3. Dehydrate snap peas for 8 hours.

Nutritional Value (Amount per Serving):

- Calories 59
- Fat 0.3 g
- Carbohydrates 10.5 g
- Sugar 4.1 g
- Protein 3.9 g
- Cholesterol 0 mg

Salmon Jerky

Prep Time	Cook Time	Serving
10 Minutes	4 hours	6

Ingredients

- 1 1/4 lbs salmon, cut into 1/4-inch slices
- 1 1/2 tbsp fresh lemon juice
- 1 tbsp molasses
- 1/2 cup soy sauce
- 1/2 tsp liquid smoke
- 1 1/4 tsp black pepper

Directions

1. In a bowl, mix together liquid smoke, black pepper, lemon juice, molasses, and soy sauce.
2. Add sliced salmon into the bowl and mix well. Cover bowl and place in the refrigerator overnight.
3. Remove salmon slices from marinade and arrange on the dehydrate basket in a single layer.
4. Insert wire rack in rack position 4. Select DEHYDRATE, set temperature 145 F, timer for 4 hours. Press start.
5. Dehydrate salmon slices for 4 hours.

Nutritional Value (Amount per Serving):
- Calories 148
- Fat 5.9 g
- Carbohydrates 4.5 g
- Sugar 2.3 g
- Protein 19.7 g
- Cholesterol 42 mg

Chicken Jerky

Prep Time	Cook Time	Serving
10 Minutes	7 hours	4

Ingredients

- 1 1/2 lb chicken tenders, boneless, skinless and cut into 1/4 inch strips
- 1/2 tsp garlic powder
- 1 tsp lemon juice
- 1/2 cup soy sauce
- 1/4 tsp ground ginger
- 1/4 tsp black pepper

Directions

1. Mix all ingredients except chicken into the zip-lock bag. Add chicken and seal bag and place in the refrigerator for 30 minutes.
2. Arrange marinated meat slices on the dehydrate basket in a single layer.
3. Insert wire rack in rack position 4. Select DEHYDRATE, set temperature 145 F, timer for 7 hours. Press start.
4. Dehydrate meat slices for 7 hours.

Nutritional Value (Amount per Serving):
- Calories 342
- Fat 12.6 g
- Carbohydrates 2.9 g
- Sugar 0.7 g
- Protein 51.3 g
- Cholesterol 151 mg

Garlicky Jerky

Prep Time	Cook Time	Serving
10 Minutes	4 hours	8

Ingredients

- 3 lbs flank steak, cut into 1/4-inch thick slices
- 1/4 cup coconut amino
- 1 1/2 tbsp garlic powder

Directions

1. In a bowl, mix together garlic powder and coconut amino. Add meat slices into the bowl and mix until well coated. Cover bowl and place in the refrigerator overnight.
2. Arrange marinated meat slices on the dehydrate basket in a single layer.
3. Insert wire rack in rack position 4. Select DEHYDRATE, set temperature 145 F, timer for 4 hours. Press start.
4. Dehydrate meat slices for 4 hours.

Nutritional Value (Amount per Serving):
- Calories 343
- Fat 14.2 g
- Carbohydrates 2.7 g
- Sugar 0.4 g
- Protein 47.6 g
- Cholesterol 94 mg

Chapter 8 Dehydrated

Dehydrated Bell Peppers

Prep Time	Cook Time	Serving
10 Minutes	24 hours	4

Ingredients

- 4 bell peppers, remove seeds and cut into 1/2-inch chunks

Directions

1. Arrange bell peppers chunks on the dehydrate basket in a single layer.
2. Insert wire rack in rack position 4. Select DEHYDRATE, set temperature 135 F, timer for 24 hours. Press start.
3. Dehydrate bell pepper chunks for 24 hours.

Nutritional Value (Amount per Serving):
- Calories 38
- Fat 0.3 g
- Carbohydrates 9 g
- Sugar 6 g
- Protein 1.2 g
- Cholesterol 0 mg

Dehydrated Cauliflower Popcorn

Prep Time	Cook Time	Serving
10 Minutes	12 hours	4

Ingredients

- 1 cauliflower head, cut into florets
- 2 tsp chili powder
- 1 tbsp olive oil
- Salt

Directions

1. Toss cauliflower florets with chili powder, oil, and salt and arrange on the dehydrate basket in a single layer.
2. Insert wire rack in rack position 4. Select DEHYDRATE, set temperature 115 F, timer for 12 hours. Press start.
3. Dehydrate cauliflower florets for 12 hours.

Nutritional Value (Amount per Serving):
- Calories 51
- Fat 3.8 g
- Carbohydrates 4.2 g
- Sugar 1.7 g
- Protein 1.5 g
- Cholesterol 0 mg

Dehydrated Dragon Fruit Slices

Prep Time	Cook Time	Serving
10 Minutes	12 hours	4

Ingredients

- 2 dragon fruit, peel & cut into 1/4-inch thick slices

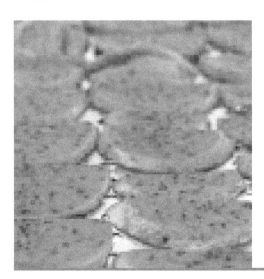

Directions

5. Insert wire rack in rack position 4. Select DEHYDRATE, set temperature 115 F, timer for 12 hours. Press start.
6. Dehydrate dragon fruit slices for 12 hours.

Nutritional Value (Amount per Serving):
- Calories 23
- Fat 0 g
- Carbohydrates 6 g
- Sugar 6 g
- Protein 0 g
- Cholesterol 0 mg

Dehydrated Orange Slices

Prep Time	Cook Time	Serving
10 Minutes	12 hours	4

Ingredients

- 2 oranges, peel & cut into slices

Directions

4. Arrange orange slices on the dehydrate basket in a single layer.
5. Insert wire rack in rack position 4. Select DEHYDRATE, set temperature 135 F, timer for 12 hours. Press start.
6. Dehydrate orange slices for 12 hours.

Nutritional Value (Amount per Serving):

- Calories 43
- Fat 0.1 g
- Carbohydrates 10.8 g
- Sugar 8.6 g
- Protein 0.9 g
- Cholesterol 0 mg

Dehydrated Kiwi Slices

Prep Time	Cook Time	Serving
10 Minutes	12 hours	4

Ingredients

- 2 kiwis, peeled & cut into 1/4-inch thick slices

Directions

4. Arrange kiwi fruit slices on the dehydrate basket in a single layer.
5. Insert wire rack in rack position 4. Select DEHYDRATE, set temperature 135 F, timer for 12 hours. Press start.
6. Dehydrate kiwi slices for 12 hours.

Nutritional Value (Amount per Serving):

- Calories 23
- Fat 0.2 g
- Carbohydrates 5.6 g
- Sugar 3.4 g
- Protein 0.4 g
- Cholesterol 0 mg

Dehydrated Cinnamon Zucchini Slices

Prep Time	Cook Time	Serving
10 Minutes	12 hours	4

Ingredients

- 1 zucchini, sliced thinly
- 1 tsp ground cinnamon

Directions

4. Arrange zucchini slices on the dehydrate basket in a single layer. Sprinkle with cinnamon.
5. Insert wire rack in rack position 4. Select DEHYDRATE, set temperature 135 F, timer for 12 hours. Press start.
6. Dehydrate zucchini slices for 12 hours.

Nutritional Value (Amount per Serving):

- Calories 9
- Fat 0.1 g
- Carbohydrates 2.1 g
- Sugar 0.9 g
- Protein 0.6 g
- Cholesterol 0 mg

Dehydrated Cinnamon Apple Slices

Prep Time	Cook Time	Serving
10 Minutes	8 hours	4

Ingredients

- 2 apples, cut into 1/8-inch thick slices
- 1 tsp ground cinnamon

Directions

4. Arrange apple slices on the dehydrate basket in a single layer. Sprinkle cinnamon on apple slices.
5. Insert wire rack in rack position 4. Select DEHYDRATE, set temperature 135 F, timer for 8 hours. Press start.
6. Dehydrate apple slices for 8 hours.

Nutritional Value (Amount per Serving):

- Calories 59
- Fat 0.2 g
- Carbohydrates 15.9 g
- Sugar 11.6 g
- Protein 0.3 g
- Cholesterol 0 mg

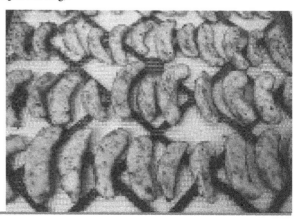

Dehydrated Spicy Eggplant Slices

Prep Time	Cook Time	Serving
10 Minutes	6 hours	2

Ingredients

- 1 medium eggplant, cut into 1/4-inch thick slices
- 2 tsp paprika
- Salt

Directions

4. Arrange eggplant slices on the dehydrate basket in a single layer. Season with salt.
5. Insert wire rack in rack position 4. Select DEHYDRATE, set temperature 140 F, timer for 6 hours. Press start.
6. Dehydrate eggplant slices for 6 hours.

Nutritional Value (Amount per Serving):
- Calories 63
- Fat 0.7 g
- Carbohydrates 14.6 g
- Sugar 7.1 g
- Protein 2.6 g
- Cholesterol 0 mg

Dehydrated Banana Slices

Prep Time	Cook Time	Serving
10 Minutes	6 hours	2

Ingredients

- 2 bananas, peel & cut into 1/8-inch thick slices

Directions

4. Arrange banana slices on the dehydrate basket in a single layer.
5. Insert wire rack in rack position 4. Select DEHYDRATE, set temperature 135 F, timer for 6 hours. Press start.
6. Dehydrate banana slices for 6 hours.

Nutritional Value (Amount per Serving):
- Calories 105
- Fat 0.4 g
- Carbohydrates 27 g
- Sugar 14.4 g
- Protein 1.3 g
- Cholesterol 0 mg

Dehydrated Chickpeas

Prep Time	Cook Time	Serving
10 Minutes	10 hours	4

Ingredients

- 10 oz can chickpeas, drained and rinsed
- Salt

Directions

4. Arrange chickpeas on the dehydrate basket in a single layer. Season with salt.
5. Insert wire rack in rack position 4. Select DEHYDRATE, set temperature 135 F, timer for 10 hours. Press start.
6. Dehydrate chickpeas for 10 hours.

Nutritional Value (Amount per Serving):
- Calories 84
- Fat 0.8 g
- Carbohydrates 16 g
- Sugar 0 g
- Protein 3.5 g
- Cholesterol 0 mg

Dehydrated Pineapple Chunks

Prep Time	Cook Time	Serving
10 Minutes	12 hours	2

Ingredients

- 1 cup pineapple chunks

Directions

4. Arrange pineapple chunks on the dehydrate basket in a single layer.
5. Insert wire rack in rack position 4. Select DEHYDRATE, set temperature 135 F, timer for 12 hours. Press start.
6. Dehydrate pineapple chunks for 12 hours.

Nutritional Value (Amount per Serving):
- Calories 41
- Fat 0.1 g
- Carbohydrates 10.8 g
- Sugar 8.1 g
- Protein 0.4 g
- Cholesterol 0 mg

Dehydrated Summer Squash Chips

Prep Time	Cook Time	Serving
10 Minutes	10 hours	2

Ingredients

- 1 yellow summer squash, sliced thinly
- Pepper
- Salt

Directions

4. Arrange squash slices on the dehydrate basket in a single layer. Season with pepper & salt.
5. Insert wire rack in rack position 4. Select DEHYDRATE, set temperature 115 F, timer for 10 hours. Press start.
6. Dehydrate squash slices for 10 hours.

Nutritional Value (Amount per Serving):
- Calories 7
- Fat 0 g
- Carbohydrates 1.8 g
- Sugar 0.8 g
- Protein 0.3 g
- Cholesterol 0 mg

Dehydrated Okra

Prep Time	Cook Time	Serving
10 Minutes	24 hours	2

Ingredients

- 6 pods okra, slice into rounds

Directions

4. Arrange okra slices on the dehydrate basket in a single layer.
5. Insert wire rack in rack position 4. Select DEHYDRATE, set temperature 130 F, timer for 24 hours. Press start.
6. Dehydrate okra slices for 24 hours.

Nutritional Value (Amount per Serving):
- Calories 54
- Fat 0.6 g
- Carbohydrates 10.8 g
- Sugar 5.7 g
- Protein 4.5 g
- Cholesterol 0 mg

Dehydrated Lemon Slices

Prep Time	Cook Time	Serving
10 Minutes	10 hours	4

Ingredients

- 2 lemons, cut into 1/4-inch thick slices

Directions

4. Arrange lemon slices on the dehydrate basket in a single layer.
5. Insert wire rack in rack position 4. Select DEHYDRATE, set temperature 125 F, timer for 10 hours. Press start.
6. Dehydrate lemon slices for 10 hours.

Nutritional Value (Amount per Serving):
- Calories 8
- Fat 0.1 g
- Carbohydrates 2.7 g
- Sugar 0.7 g
- Protein 0.3 g
- Cholesterol 0 mg

Dehydrated Pear Slices

Prep Time	Cook Time	Serving
10 Minutes	5 hours	4

Ingredients

- 2 pears, cut into 1/4-inch thick slices

Directions

4. Arrange pear slices on the dehydrate basket in a single layer.
5. Insert wire rack in rack position 4. Select DEHYDRATE, set temperature 160 F, timer for 5 hours. Press start.
6. Dehydrate pear slices for 5 hours.

Nutritional Value (Amount per Serving):
- Calories 60
- Fat 0.2 g
- Carbohydrates 15.9 g
- Sugar 10.2 g
- Protein 0.4 g
- Cholesterol 0 mg

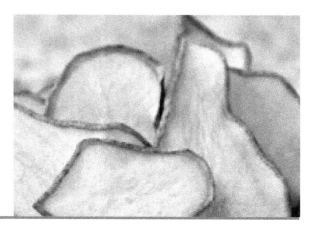

Dehydrated Mushroom Chips

Prep Time	Cook Time	Serving
10 Minutes	5 hours	2

Ingredients

- 1 cup mushrooms, clean and cut into 1/8-inch thick slices
- Salt

Directions

4. Arrange mushroom slices on the dehydrate basket in a single layer. Season with salt.
5. Insert wire rack in rack position 4. Select DEHYDRATE, set temperature 160 F, timer for 5 hours. Press start.
6. Dehydrate mushroom slices for 5 hours.

Nutritional Value (Amount per Serving):
- Calories 4
- Fat 0.1 g
- Carbohydrates 0.6 g
- Sugar 0.3 g
- Protein 0.6 g
- Cholesterol 0 mg

Dehydrated Snap Peas

Prep Time	Cook Time	Serving
10 Minutes	8 hours	4

Ingredients

- 2 cups snap peas
- Salt

Directions

4. Arrange snap peas on the dehydrate basket in a single layer. Season with salt.
5. Insert wire rack in rack position 4. Select DEHYDRATE, set temperature 135 F, timer for 8 hours. Press start.
6. Dehydrate snap peas for 8 hours.

Nutritional Value (Amount per Serving):
- Calories 59
- Fat 0.3 g
- Carbohydrates 10.5 g
- Sugar 4.1 g
- Protein 3.9 g
- Cholesterol 0 mg

Salmon Jerky

Prep Time	Cook Time	Serving
10 Minutes	4 hours	6

Ingredients

- 1 1/4 lbs salmon, cut into 1/4-inch slices
- 1 1/2 tbsp fresh lemon juice
- 1 tbsp molasses
- 1/2 cup soy sauce
- 1/2 tsp liquid smoke
- 1 1/4 tsp black pepper

Directions

6. In a bowl, mix together liquid smoke, black pepper, lemon juice, molasses, and soy sauce.
7. Add sliced salmon into the bowl and mix well. Cover bowl and place in the refrigerator overnight.
8. Remove salmon slices from marinade and arrange on the dehydrate basket in a single layer.
9. Insert wire rack in rack position 4. Select DEHYDRATE, set temperature 145 F, timer for 4 hours. Press start.
10. Dehydrate salmon slices for 4 hours.

Nutritional Value (Amount per Serving):
- Calories 148
- Fat 5.9 g
- Carbohydrates 4.5 g
- Sugar 2.3 g
- Protein 19.7 g
- Cholesterol 42 mg

Chicken Jerky

Prep Time	Cook Time	Serving
10 Minutes	7 hours	4

Ingredients

- 1 1/2 lb chicken tenders, boneless, skinless and cut into 1/4 inch strips
- 1/2 tsp garlic powder
- 1 tsp lemon juice
- 1/2 cup soy sauce
- 1/4 tsp ground ginger
- 1/4 tsp black pepper

Directions

5. Mix all ingredients except chicken into the zip-lock bag. Add chicken and seal bag and place in the refrigerator for 30 minutes.
6. Arrange marinated meat slices on the dehydrate basket in a single layer.
7. Insert wire rack in rack position 4. Select DEHYDRATE, set temperature 145 F, timer for 7 hours. Press start.
8. Dehydrate meat slices for 7 hours.

Nutritional Value (Amount per Serving):
- Calories 342
- Fat 12.6 g
- Carbohydrates 2.9 g
- Sugar 0.7 g
- Protein 51.3 g
- Cholesterol 151 mg

Garlicky Jerky

Prep Time	Cook Time	Serving
10 Minutes	4 hours	8

Ingredients

- 3 lbs flank steak, cut into 1/4-inch thick slices
- 1/4 cup coconut amino
- 1 1/2 tbsp garlic powder

Directions

5. In a bowl, mix together garlic powder and coconut amino. Add meat slices into the bowl and mix until well coated. Cover bowl and place in the refrigerator overnight.
6. Arrange marinated meat slices on the dehydrate basket in a single layer.
7. Insert wire rack in rack position 4. Select DEHYDRATE, set temperature 145 F, timer for 4 hours. Press start.
8. Dehydrate meat slices for 4 hours.

Nutritional Value (Amount per Serving):
- Calories 343
- Fat 14.2 g
- Carbohydrates 2.7 g
- Sugar 0.4 g
- Protein 47.6 g
- Cholesterol 94 mg

Dehydrated Bell Peppers

Prep Time	Cook Time	Serving
10 Minutes	24 hours	4

Ingredients

- 4 bell peppers, remove seeds and cut into 1/2-inch chunks

Directions

4. Arrange bell peppers chunks on the dehydrate basket in a single layer.
5. Insert wire rack in rack position 4. Select DEHYDRATE, set temperature 135 F, timer for 24 hours. Press start.
6. Dehydrate bell pepper chunks for 24 hours.

Nutritional Value (Amount per Serving):
- Calories 38
- Fat 0.3 g
- Carbohydrates 9 g
- Sugar 6 g
- Protein 1.2 g
- Cholesterol 0 mg

Dehydrated Cauliflower Popcorn

Prep Time	Cook Time	Serving
10 Minutes	12 hours	4

Ingredients

- 1 cauliflower head, cut into florets
- 2 tsp chili powder
- 1 tbsp olive oil
- Salt

Directions

4. Toss cauliflower florets with chili powder, oil, and salt and arrange on the dehydrate basket in a single layer.
5. Insert wire rack in rack position 4. Select DEHYDRATE, set temperature 115 F, timer for 12 hours. Press start.
6. Dehydrate cauliflower florets for 12 hours.

Nutritional Value (Amount per Serving):
- Calories 51
- Fat 3.8 g
- Carbohydrates 4.2 g
- Sugar 1.7 g
- Protein 1.5 g
- Cholesterol 0 mg

Chapter 9 Desserts

Choco Lava Cake

Prep Time	Cook Time	Serving
10 Minutes	9 hours	2

Ingredients

- 1 egg
- 1/2 tsp baking powder
- 2 tbsp water
- 2 tbsp cocoa powder
- 1 tbsp butter, melted
- 1 tbsp flax meal
- 2 tbsp Swerve
- Pinch of salt

Directions

1. Spray 2 ramekins with cooking spray and set aside.
2. Insert wire rack in rack position 6. Select air fry, set temperature 350 F, timer for 9 minutes. Press start to preheat the oven.
3. In a bowl, whisk together all ingredients until well combined.
4. Pour batter into the prepared ramekins and bake for 9 minutes.
5. Serve and enjoy.

Nutritional Value (Amount per Serving):
- Calories 121
- Fat 11 g
- Carbohydrates 19.9 g
- Sugar 15.3 g
- Protein 4.6 g
- Cholesterol 82 mg

Baked Spiced Apples

Prep Time	Cook Time	Serving
10 Minutes	10 Minutes	6

Ingredients

- 4 apples, sliced
- 1/2 cup erythritol
- 2 tbsp butter, melted
- 1 tsp apple pie spice

Directions

1. Insert wire rack in rack position 6. Select bake, set temperature 350 F, timer for 10 minutes. Press start to preheat the oven.
2. Add apple slices in a large bowl and sprinkle with sweetener and apple pie spice. Add melted butter and toss to coat.
3. Transfer apple slices in a baking dish and air fry for 10 minutes.
4. Serve and enjoy.

Nutritional Value (Amount per Serving):
- Calories 73
- Fat 4.6 g
- Carbohydrates 8.2 g
- Sugar 5.4 g
- Protein 0 g
- Cholesterol 0 mg

Cheesecake

Prep Time	Cook Time	Serving
10 Minutes	10 Minutes	2

Ingredients

- 2 eggs
- 16 oz cream cheese, softened
- 2 tbsp sour cream
- 1/2 tsp fresh lemon juice
- 1 tsp vanilla

Directions

1. Insert wire rack in rack position 6. Select air fry, set temperature 350 F, timer for 10 minutes. Press start to preheat the oven.
2. Add eggs, lemon juice, vanilla, and sweetener in a large bowl and beat until smooth.
3. Add cream cheese and sour cream and beat until fluffy.
4. Pour batter into the 2 4-inch springform pan and cook for 10 minutes.
5. Place in refrigerator overnight.
6. Serve and enjoy.

Nutritional Value (Amount per Serving):
- Calories 886
- Fat 86 g
- Carbohydrates 97.2 g
- Sugar 91.1 g
- Protein 23.1 g
- Cholesterol 418 mg

Delicious Cream Cheese Muffins

Prep Time	Cook Time	Serving
10 Minutes	16 Minutes	10

Ingredients

- 2 eggs
- 1 tsp ground cinnamon
- 1/2 tsp vanilla
- 1/2 cup erythritol
- 8 oz cream cheese

Directions

1. Insert wire rack in rack position 6. Select bake, set temperature 325 F, timer for 16 minutes. Press start to preheat the oven.
2. In a bowl, mix together cream cheese, vanilla, erythritol, and eggs until soft.
3. Pour batter into the silicone muffin molds and sprinkle cinnamon on top.
4. Cook for 16 minutes.
5. Serve and enjoy.

Nutritional Value (Amount per Serving):
- Calories 90
- Fat 8.8 g
- Carbohydrates 13 g
- Sugar 12.2 g
- Protein 2.8 g
- Cholesterol 58 mg

Almond Cinnamon Muffins

Prep Time	Cook Time	Serving
10 Minutes	12 Minutes	20

Ingredients

- 1/2 cup almond flour
- 1/2 cup coconut oil
- 1/2 cup pumpkin puree
- 1 tbsp cinnamon
- 1 tsp baking powder
- 2 scoops vanilla protein powder
- 1/2 cup almond butter

Directions

1. Insert wire rack in rack position 6. Select air fry, set temperature 325 F, timer for 12 minutes. Press start to preheat the oven.
2. In a large bowl, mix together all dry ingredients.
3. Add wet ingredients into the dry ingredients and mix until well combined.
4. Pour batter into the silicone muffin molds and cook for 12 minutes.
5. Serve and enjoy.

Nutritional Value (Amount per Serving):
- Calories 80
- Fat 7.1 g
- Carbohydrates 1 g
- Sugar 0.4 g
- Protein 3 g
- Cholesterol 0 mg

Almond Pumpkin Muffins

Prep Time	Cook Time	Serving
10 Minutes	120 Minutes	10

Ingredients

- 4 large eggs
- 2/3 cup erythritol
- 1 tsp vanilla
- 1/3 cup coconut oil, melted
- 1/2 cup almond flour
- 1/2 cup pumpkin puree
- 1 tbsp pumpkin pie spice
- 1 tbsp baking powder
- 1/2 cup coconut flour
- 1/2 tsp sea salt

Directions

1. Insert wire rack in rack position 6. Select air fry, set temperature 325 F, timer for 20 minutes. Press start to preheat the oven.
2. In a large bowl, mix together coconut flour, pumpkin pie spice, baking powder, erythritol, almond flour, and sea salt.
3. Stir in eggs, vanilla, coconut oil, and pumpkin puree until well combined.
4. Pour batter into the silicone muffin molds and cook muffins for 20 minutes.
5. Serve and enjoy.

Nutritional Value (Amount per Serving):

- Calories 150
- Fat 13 g
- Carbohydrates 7 g
- Sugar 2 g
- Protein 5 g
- Cholesterol 75 mg

Healthy Blueberry Muffins

Prep Time	Cook Time	Serving
10 Minutes	20 Minutes	12

Ingredients

- 3 large eggs
- 2 1/2 cups almond flour
- 3/4 cup blueberries
- 1/2 tsp vanilla
- 1/3 cup almond milk
- 1/3 cup coconut oil, melted
- 1 1/2 tsp gluten-free baking powder
- 1/2 cup erythritol

Directions

1. Insert wire rack in rack position 6. Select air fry, set temperature 325 F, timer for 20 minutes. Press start to preheat the oven.
2. In a large bowl, mix together almond flour, baking powder, erythritol.
3. Stir in the coconut oil, vanilla, eggs, and almond milk.
4. Add blueberries and fold well.
5. Pour batter into the silicone muffin molds and cook muffins for 20 minutes.
6. Serve and enjoy.

Nutritional Value (Amount per Serving):

- Calories 215
- Fat 19 g
- Carbohydrates 5 g
- Sugar 2 g
- Protein 7 g
- Cholesterol 45 mg

Choco Almond Butter Brownie

Prep Time	Cook Time	Serving
10 Minutes	16 Minutes	4

Ingredients

- 1 cup bananas, overripe
- 1/2 cup almond butter, melted
- 1 scoop protein powder
- 2 tbsp cocoa powder

Directions

1. Insert wire rack in rack position 6. Select air fry, set temperature 350 F, timer for 16 minutes. Press start to preheat the oven.
2. Spray baking dish with cooking spray.
3. Add all ingredients into the blender and blend until smooth.
4. Pour batter into the prepared baking dish and cook brownie for 16 minutes.
5. Serve and enjoy.

Nutritional Value (Amount per Serving):

- Calories 80
- Fat 2.1 g
- Carbohydrates 11.4 g
- Protein 7 g
- Sugars 5 g
- Cholesterol 15 mg

Vanilla Coconut Pie

Prep Time	Cook Time	Serving
10 Minutes	12 Minutes	6

Ingredients

- 2 eggs
- 1 1/2 tsp vanilla
- 1/4 cup butter
- 1 1/2 cups coconut milk
- 1/2 cup coconut flour
- 1/2 cup Swerve
- 1 cup shredded coconut

Directions

1. Spray a 6-inch baking dish with cooking spray and set aside.
2. Insert wire rack in rack position 6. Select bake, set temperature 350 F, timer for 12 minutes. Press start to preheat the oven.
3. Add all ingredients into the large bowl and mix until well combined.
4. Pour batter into the prepared dish and cook for 10-12 minutes.
5. Slice and serve.

Nutritional Value (Amount per Serving):

- Calories 317
- Fat 28.9 g
- Carbohydrates 32.3 g
- Sugar 23.1 g
- Protein 5.1 g
- Cholesterol 75 mg

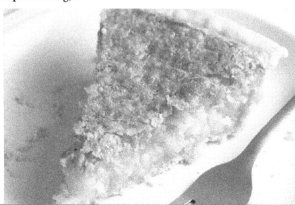

Moist Chocolate Brownies

Prep Time	Cook Time	Serving
10 Minutes	35 Minutes	9

Ingredients

- 2 eggs
- 1 tsp baking powder
- 4 tbsp coconut oil, melted
- 2/3 cup unsweetened cocoa powder
- 2 avocados, mashed
- 2 tbsp swerve
- 1/3 cup chocolate chips, melted

Directions

1. Insert wire rack in rack position 6. Select bake, set temperature 325 F, timer for 35 minutes. Press start to preheat the oven.
2. In a mixing bowl, mix together all dry ingredients.
3. In another bowl, mix together avocado and eggs until well combined.
4. Add dry mixture to the wet along with melted chocolate and oil. Mix well.
5. Pour batter in a baking dish and bake for 35 minutes.
6. Slice and serve.

Nutritional Value (Amount per Serving):
- Calories 207
- Fat 18 g
- Carbohydrates 11 g
- Sugar 3.6 g
- Protein 3.8 g
- Cholesterol 38 mg

Peanut Butter Choco Cookies

Prep Time	Cook Time	Serving
10 Minutes	10 Minutes	24

Ingredients

- 2 eggs
- 2 tbsp unsweetened cocoa powder
- 1 tsp baking soda
- 2 tsp vanilla
- 1 tbsp butter, melted
- 1 cup peanut butter
- 2/3 cup erythritol
- 1 1/3 cups almond flour

Directions

1. Line baking sheet with parchment paper and set aside.
2. Insert wire rack in rack position 6. Select bake, set temperature 350 F, timer for 10 minutes. Press start to preheat the oven.
3. Add all ingredients into the mixing bowl and stir to combine.
4. Make 2-inch balls from mixture and place on a baking sheet and gently press down each ball with a fork.
5. Bake for 10 minutes.
6. Serve and enjoy.

Nutritional Value (Amount per Serving):
- Calories 110
- Fat 9 g
- Carbohydrates 9 g
- Sugar 1.3 g
- Protein 4.6 g
- Cholesterol 15 mg

Baked Chocolate Macaroon

Prep Time	Cook Time	Serving
10 Minutes	20 Minutes	20

Ingredients

- 2 eggs
- 1/3 cup coconut, shredded
- 1/3 cup erythritol
- 1/2 tsp baking powder
- 1 tsp vanilla
- 1/4 cup coconut oil
- 1/4 cup cocoa powder
- 3 tbsp coconut flour
- 1 cup almond flour
- Pinch of salt

Directions

1. Line baking sheet with parchment paper and set aside.
2. Insert wire rack in rack position 6. Select bake, set temperature 375 F, timer for 30 minutes. Press start to preheat the oven.
3. Add all ingredients into the mixing bowl and mix until well combined.
4. Make small balls from mixture and place on a baking sheet.
5. Bake for 20 minutes.
6. Serve and enjoy.

Nutritional Value (Amount per Serving):

- Calories 80
- Fat 7 g
- Carbohydrates 6.5 g
- Sugar 0.5 g
- Protein 2.3 g
- Cholesterol 16 mg

Choco Almond Cookies

Prep Time	Cook Time	Serving
10 Minutes	10 Minutes	20

Ingredients

- 2 tbsp chocolate protein powder
- 3 tbsp ground chia
- 1 cup almond flour
- 1 cup sunflower seed butter

Directions

1. Line baking sheet with parchment paper and set aside.
2. Insert wire rack in rack position 6. Select bake, set temperature 350 F, timer for 10 minutes. Press start to preheat the oven.
3. In a large bowl, add all ingredients and mix until combined.
4. Make small balls from mixture and place on a prepared baking sheet and press lightly down with the back of a fork.
5. Bake for 10 minutes.
6. Serve and enjoy.

Nutritional Value (Amount per Serving):

- Calories 90
- Fat 7 g
- Carbohydrates 4.1 g
- Sugar 0.1 g
- Protein 4.3 g
- Cholesterol 0 mg

Pecan Cookies

Prep Time	Cook Time	Serving
10 Minutes	20 Minutes	15

Ingredients

- 1 cup pecans
- 2/3 cup Swerve
- 1/3 cup coconut flour
- 1 cup almond flour
- 1/2 cup butter
- 1 tsp vanilla
- 2 tsp gelatin

Directions

1. Line baking sheet with parchment paper and set aside.
2. Insert wire rack in rack position 6. Select bake, set temperature 350 F, timer for 20 minutes. Press start to preheat the oven.
3. Add butter, vanilla, gelatine, swerve, coconut flour, and almond flour into the food processor and process until crumbs form.
4. Add pecans and process until chopped.
5. Make 15 cookies from mixture and place onto a prepared baking sheet and bake for 20 minutes.
6. Serve and enjoy.

Nutritional Value (Amount per Serving):
- Calories 113
- Fat 11.7 g
- Carbohydrates 1.7 g
- Sugar 0.4 g
- Protein 1.2 g
- Cholesterol 15 mg

Delicious Pumpkin Cookies

Prep Time	Cook Time	Serving
10 Minutes	25 Minutes	25

Ingredients

- 1 egg
- 1 tsp vanilla
- 1/2 cup butter
- 1/2 cup pumpkin puree
- 2 cups almond flour
- 1 tsp liquid stevia
- 1/2 tsp pumpkin pie spice
- 1/2 tsp baking powder

Directions

1. Line baking sheet with parchment paper and set aside.
2. Insert wire rack in rack position 6. Select bake, set temperature 320 F, timer for 25 minutes. Press start to preheat the oven.
3. In a large bowl, add all ingredients and mix until well combined.
4. Make 25 cookies from mixture and place onto a prepared baking sheet and bake for 25 minutes.
5. Serve and enjoy.

Nutritional Value (Amount per Serving):
- Calories 46
- Fat 4.6 g
- Carbohydrates 0.9 g
- Sugar 0.3 g
- Protein 0.7 g
- Cholesterol 15 mg

Cinnamon Pumpkin Pie

Prep Time	Cook Time	Serving
10 Minutes	30 Minutes	4

Ingredients

- 3 eggs
- 1/2 cup cream
- 1/2 cup almond milk
- 1/2 cup pumpkin puree
- 1/2 tsp cinnamon
- 1 tsp vanilla
- 1/4 cup Swerve

Directions

1. Spray a square baking dish with cooking spray and set aside.
2. Insert wire rack in rack position 6. Select bake, set temperature 350 F, timer for 30 minutes. Press start to preheat the oven.
3. In a large bowl, add all ingredients and whisk until smooth.
4. Pour pie mixture into the prepared dish and bake for 30 minutes.
5. Remove from oven and set aside to cool completely.
6. Place into the refrigerator for 2 hours.
7. Sliced and serve.

Nutritional Value (Amount per Serving):
- Calories 86
- Fat 5.5 g
- Carbohydrates 4.4 g
- Sugar 2 g
- Protein 4.9 g
- Cholesterol 128 mg

Baked Apple Bars

Prep Time	Cook Time	Serving
10 Minutes	45 Minutes	8

Ingredients

- 1/4 cup dried apples
- 1/4 cup coconut butter, softened
- 1 cup pecans
- 1 cup of water
- 1 tsp vanilla
- 1 1/2 tsp baking powder
- 1 1/2 tsp cinnamon
- 1 tbsp ground flax seed
- 2 tbsp swerve

Directions

1. Spray 8*8-inch square dish with cooking spray and set aside.
2. Insert wire rack in rack position 6. Select bake, set temperature 350 F, timer for 45 minutes. Press start to preheat the oven.
3. Add all ingredients into the blender and blend until smooth.
4. Pour blended mixture into the prepared dish and bake for 40-45 minutes,
5. Slice and serve.

Nutritional Value (Amount per Serving):
- Calories 160
- Fat 14.8 g
- Carbohydrates 6.3 g
- Sugar 1.8 g
- Protein 2.2 g
- Cholesterol 0 mg

Ricotta Cheese Cake

Prep Time	Cook Time	Serving
10 Minutes	55 Minutes	8

Ingredients

- 4 eggs
- 1 fresh lemon zest
- 2 tbsp stevia
- 18 oz ricotta
- 1 fresh lemon juice

Directions

1. Spray cake pan with cooking spray and set aside.
2. Insert wire rack in rack position 6. Select bake, set temperature 350 F, timer for 55 minutes. Press start to preheat the oven.
3. In a large mixing bowl, beat ricotta until smooth.
4. Add egg one by one and whisk well.
5. Add lemon juice, lemon zest, and stevia and mix well.
6. Transfer mixture into the prepared cake pan and bake for 55 minutes.
7. Remove cake from oven and set aside to cool completely.
8. Place cake in the refrigerator for 2 hours.
9. Slices and serve.

Nutritional Value (Amount per Serving):
- Calories 120
- Fat 7.1 g
- Carbohydrates 5 g
- Sugar 1.1 g
- Protein 9.9 g
- Cholesterol 101 mg

Easy Pound Cake

Prep Time	Cook Time	Serving
10 Minutes	35 Minutes	9

Ingredients

- 5 eggs
- 1 tsp orange extract
- 1 cup Splenda
- 4 oz cream cheese, softened
- 1/2 cup butter, softened
- 1 tsp baking powder
- 7 oz almond flour
- 1 tsp vanilla

Directions

1. Spray 9-inch cake pan with cooking spray and set aside.
2. Insert wire rack in rack position 6. Select bake, set temperature 350 F, timer for 35 minutes. Press start to preheat the oven.
3. Add all ingredients into the mixing bowl and mix until batter is fluffy.
4. Pour batter into the prepared pan and bake for 35 minutes.
5. Remove cake from oven and set aside to cool completely.
6. Slices and serve.

Nutritional Value (Amount per Serving):
- Calories 287
- Fat 27.2 g
- Carbohydrates 5.2 g
- Sugar 1 g
- Protein 8.5 g
- Cholesterol 132 mg

Moist Almond Choco Muffins

Prep Time	Cook Time	Serving
10 Minutes	30 Minutes	8

Ingredients

- 2 eggs
- 1/2 cup cocoa powder
- 1 cup ground almonds
- 1/2 cup cream
- 1 tsp vanilla extract
- 4 tbsp Swerve

Directions

1. Line muffin pan with cupcake liners and set aside.
2. Insert wire rack in rack position 6. Select bake, set temperature 375 F, timer for 30 minutes. Press start to preheat the oven.
3. In a bowl, mix together all dry ingredients.
4. In another bowl, beat together eggs, vanilla, and cream.
5. Pour egg mixture into the dry ingredients and mix well to combine.
6. Pour batter into the prepared muffin pan and bake for 30 minutes.
7. Serve and enjoy.

Nutritional Value (Amount per Serving):
- Calories 86
- Fat 6.9 g
- Carbohydrates 9.7 g
- Protein 4 g
- Sugar 0.8 g
- Cholesterol 35mg

Fluffy Baked Donuts

Prep Time	Cook Time	Serving
10 Minutes	15 Minutes	12

Ingredients

- 2 eggs
- 1/2 cup buttermilk
- 1/4 cup vegetable oil
- 1 cup all-purpose flour
- 1/2 tsp vanilla
- 1 tsp baking powder
- 3/4 cup sugar
- 1/2 tsp salt

Directions

1. Insert wire rack in rack position 6. Select bake, set temperature 350 F, timer for 15 minutes. Press start to preheat the oven.
2. Spray donut pan with cooking spray and set aside.
3. In a bowl, mix together oil, vanilla, baking powder, sugar, eggs, buttermilk, and salt until well combined. Stir in flour and mix until smooth.
4. Pour batter into the prepared donut pan and bake for 15 minutes.
5. Serve and enjoy.

Nutritional Value (Amount per Serving):
- Calories 140
- Fat 5.5 g
- Carbohydrates 21.2 g
- Sugar 13.1 g
- Protein 2.3 g
- Cholesterol 28 mg

Eggless Brownies

Prep Time	Cook Time	Serving
10 Minutes	40 Minutes	8

Ingredients

- 1/4 cup walnuts, chopped
- 1/2 cup butter, melted
- 1/3 cup cocoa powder
- 2 tsp baking powder
- 1 cup of sugar
- 1/2 cup chocolate chips
- 2 tsp vanilla
- 1 tbsp milk
- 3/4 cup yogurt
- 1 cup all-purpose flour
- 1/4 tsp salt

Directions

1. Spray an 8*8-inch baking dish with cooking spray.
2. Insert wire rack in rack position 6. Select bake, set temperature 350 F, timer for 40 minutes. Press start to preheat the oven.
3. In a large mixing bowl, sift flour, cocoa powder, baking powder, and salt. Mix well and set aside.
4. In another bowl, add butter, vanilla, milk, and yogurt and whisk until well combined.
5. Add flour mixture into the butter mixture and mix until just combined. Fold in walnuts and chocolate chips.
6. Pour batter into the prepared baking dish and bake for 40 minutes.
7. Slice and serve.

Nutritional Value (Amount per Serving):
- Calories 362
- Fat 17.9 g
- Carbohydrates 48 g
- Sugar 32.4 g
- Protein 5.5 g
- Cholesterol 34 mg

Healthy Banana Brownies

Prep Time	Cook Time	Serving
10 Minutes	20 Minutes	12

Ingredients

- 1 egg
- 2 medium bananas, mashed
- 4 oz white chocolate
- 1 cup all-purpose flour
- 1 tsp vanilla
- 1/2 cup sugar
- 1/4 cup butter
- 1/4 tsp salt

Directions

1. Insert wire rack in rack position 6. Select bake, set temperature 350 F, timer for 20 minutes. Press start to preheat the oven.
2. Add white chocolate and butter in microwave-safe bowl and microwave for 30 seconds. Stir until melted.
3. Stir in sugar. Add mashed bananas, eggs, vanilla, and salt and mix until combined.
4. Add flour and stir to combine.
5. Pour batter into the square baking dish and bake for 20 minutes.
6. Serve and enjoy.

Nutritional Value (Amount per Serving):
- Calories 178
- Fat 7.4 g
- Carbohydrates 26.4 g
- Sugar 16.4 g
- Protein 2.3 g
- Cholesterol 26 mg

Simple Choco Cookies

Prep Time	Cook Time	Serving
10 Minutes	8 Minutes	30

Ingredients

- 3 egg whites
- 1 3/4 cup confectioner sugar
- 1 1/2 tsp vanilla extract
- 3/4 cup cocoa powder, unsweetened

Directions

1. Spray a baking sheet with cooking spray and set aside.
2. Insert wire rack in rack position 6. Select bake, set temperature 350 F, timer for 8 minutes. Press start to preheat the oven.
3. In a mixing bowl, whip egg whites until fluffy soft peaks. Slowly add in cocoa, sugar, and vanilla.
4. Drop teaspoonful onto a baking sheet into 30 small cookies.
5. Bake for 8 minutes.
6. Serve and enjoy.

Nutritional Value (Amount per Serving):
- Calories 132
- Fat 1.1 g
- Carbohydrates 30.9 g
- Sugar 0.3 g
- Protein 2.8 g
- Cholesterol 0 mg

Simple Butter Cake

Prep Time	Cook Time	Serving
10 Minutes	30 Minutes	8

Ingredients

- 1 egg, beaten
- 3/4 cup sugar
- 1/2 cup butter, softened
- 1 cup all-purpose flour
- 1/2 tsp vanilla

Directions

1. Insert wire rack in rack position 6. Select bake, set temperature 350 F, timer for 30 minutes. Press start to preheat the oven.
2. In a mixing bowl, mix together sugar and butter.
3. Add egg, flour, and vanilla and mix until combined.
4. Pour batter into an 8*8-inch square baking pan and bake for 30 minutes.
5. Slice and serve.

Nutritional Value (Amount per Serving):
- Calories 211
- Fat 10.9 g
- Carbohydrates 27.4 g
- Sugar 16.8 g
- Protein 2.2 g
- Cholesterol 45 mg

Chocolate Chip Cookies

Prep Time	Cook Time	Serving
10 Minutes	10 Minutes	30

Ingredients

- 1 egg
- 12 oz chocolate chips
- 1 tsp vanilla
- 1 cup butter, softened
- 2 cups self-rising flour
- 1/2 cup brown sugar
- 2/3 cup sugar

Directions

1. Spray cookie sheet with cooking spray and set aside.
2. Insert wire rack in rack position 6. Select bake, set temperature 375 F, timer for 10 minutes. Press start to preheat the oven.
3. Add butter, vanilla, and egg in a large mixing bowl and beat until combined.
4. Add brown sugar and sugar and beat until creamy.
5. Add flour and mix until just combined. Fold in chocolate chips.
6. Scoop out cookie dough balls onto a prepared cookie sheet.
7. Bake for 10 minutes.
8. Serve and enjoy.

Nutritional Value (Amount per Serving):

- Calories 174
- Fat 9.7 g
- Carbohydrates 19.9 g
- Sugar 12.7 g
- Protein 2 g
- Cholesterol 24 mg

Almond Butter Brownies

Prep Time	Cook Time	Serving
10 Minutes	20 Minutes	4

Ingredients

- 1 scoop protein powder
- 2 tbsp cocoa powder
- 1/2 cup almond butter, melted
- 1 cup bananas, overripe

Directions

1. Spray brownie pan with cooking spray.
2. Insert wire rack in rack position 6. Select bake, set temperature 350 F, timer for 20 minutes. Press start to preheat the oven.
3. Add all ingredients into the blender and blend until smooth.
4. Pour batter into the prepared pan and bake for 20 minutes.
5. Serve and enjoy.

Nutritional Value (Amount per Serving):

- Calories 82
- Fat 2.1 g
- Carbohydrates 11.4 g
- Protein 6.9 g
- Sugars 5 g
- Cholesterol 16 mg

V

Prep Time	Cook Time	Serving
10 Minutes	8 Minutes	4

Ingredients

- 4 tbsp coconut oil
- 2 cups almond flour
- 1 tsp vanilla extract
- 4 tbsp maple syrup

Directions

1. Insert wire rack in rack position 6. Select bake, set temperature 350 F, timer for 8 minutes. Press start to preheat the oven.
2. In a mixing bowl, combine together all ingredients until formed soft dough.
3. Add the dough in Madeline mold and bake for 8 minutes.
4. Serve and enjoy.

Nutritional Value (Amount per Serving):

- Calories 508
- Fat 40.2 g
- Carbohydrates 25.6 g
- Protein 12 g
- Sugars 12 g
- Cholesterol 0 mg

Oatmeal Cookies

Prep Time	Cook Time	Serving
10 Minutes	10 Minutes	20

Ingredients

- 3/4 cup almonds, sliced
- 1/2 cup grass-fed butter, melted
- 1 egg
- 1 1/2 cups rolled oats
- 1/2 cup Truvia
- 1 tsp vanilla

Directions

1. Line baking sheet with parchment paper.
2. Insert wire rack in rack position 6. Select bake, set temperature 350 F, timer for 10 minutes. Press start to preheat the oven.
3. In a bowl, whisk together egg, Truvia, vanilla, and butter until smooth.
4. Add almonds and oatmeal and mix well.
5. Drop mixture onto a prepared baking sheet and using spatula flatten each cookie.
6. Bake for 10 minutes.
7. Serve and enjoy.

Nutritional Value (Amount per Serving):

- Calories 67
- Fat 4.6 g
- Carbohydrates 6.8 g
- Protein 1.8 g
- Sugars 2.1 g
- Cholesterol 14 mg

Amaretti Biscuits

Prep Time	Cook Time	Serving
10 Minutes	15 Minutes	20

Ingredients

- 2 egg whites
- 1 1/2 cups almond flour
- 1 tsp almond extract
- 3 tbsp Swerve

Directions

1. Line baking sheet with parchment paper.
2. Insert wire rack in rack position 6. Select bake, set temperature 325 F, timer for 15 minutes. Press start to preheat the oven.
3. In a bowl, add egg whites and beat until stiff peaks form.
4. Combine swerve and almond flour together and add in beaten eggs. Add extract and mix well.
5. Spoon out batter onto prepared baking sheet and shape round biscuits.
6. Bake for 15 minutes.
7. Serve and enjoy.

Nutritional Value (Amount per Serving):
- Calories 53
- Fat 4 g
- Carbohydrates 2.2 g
- Protein 2.2 g
- Sugars 0.1g
- Cholesterol 0 mg

Apple Almond Cake

Prep Time	Cook Time	Serving
10 Minutes	40 Minutes	6

Ingredients

- 3 organic eggs
- 4 tbsp almonds, sliced
- 1/4 cup no sugar fruit butter
- 4 tbsp grass-fed butter, melted
- 1/2 cup Splenda
- 1 1/2 tsp baking powder
- 1/4 cup all-purpose flour
- 1 cup almond flour
- Pinch of salt

Directions

1. Spray round cake pan with cooking spray and set aside.
2. Insert wire rack in rack position 6. Select bake, set temperature 350 F, timer for 20 minutes. Press start to preheat the oven.
3. In a small bowl, combine together almond flour, salt, baking powder, and flour.
4. In another bowl, add eggs and beat until light yellow.
5. Add Splenda, sugar fruit butter, and melted butter and blend until smooth.
6. Add almond flour mixture and blend until well combined.
7. Pour batter into the prepared cake pan and spread evenly.
8. Sprinkle sliced almonds over the top of cake batter.
9. Bake for 20 minutes.
10. Serve and enjoy.

Nutritional Value (Amount per Serving):
- Calories 320
- Fat 16.8 g
- Carbohydrates 30.6 g
- Protein 8.2 g
- Sugars 20.5 g
- Cholesterol 92 mg

Baked Almond Donuts

Prep Time	Cook Time	Serving
10 Minutes	15 Minutes	8

Ingredients

- 2 eggs
- 1 1/2 tsp vanilla extract
- 3 tbsp maple syrup
- 1 cup almond flour
- 1/4 tsp baking soda

Directions

1. Spray donut pan with cooking spray and set aside.
2. Insert wire rack in rack position 6. Select bake, set temperature 320 F, timer for 15 minutes. Press start to preheat the oven.
3. In a large bowl, add all ingredients and mix well until smooth.
4. Pour batter into the greased donut pan and bake for 15 minutes.
5. Serve and enjoy.

Nutritional Value (Amount per Serving):

- Calories 122
- Fat 7.8 g
- Carbohydrates 8.2 g
- Protein 4.4 g
- Sugars 4.6 g
- Cholesterol 41 mg

Vanilla Butter Cake

Prep Time	Cook Time	Serving
10 Minutes	30 Minutes	8

Ingredients

- 1 egg, beaten
- 1/2 cup butter, softened
- 1 cup all-purpose flour
- 1/2 tsp vanilla extract
- 3/4 cup sugar

Directions

1. Insert wire rack in rack position 6. Select bake, set temperature 350 F, timer for 30 minutes. Press start to preheat the oven.
2. In a mixing bowl, mix together sugar and butter.
3. Add egg, flour, and vanilla and mix until combined.
4. Pour batter into an 8*8-inch square baking pan and bake for 30 minutes.
5. Slice and serve.

Nutritional Value (Amount per Serving):

- Calories 211
- Fat 10.9 g
- Carbohydrates 27.4 g
- Sugar 16.8 g
- Protein 2.2 g
- Cholesterol 45 mg

Sweet Cinnamon Cookies

Prep Time	Cook Time	Serving
10 Minutes	8 Minutes	35

Ingredients

- 1 large egg
- 1 tsp vanilla
- 1/2 cup powdered sugar
- 1/2 cup brown sugar
- 1/2 cup oil
- 1/2 cup butter, softened
- 2 1/4 cups flour
- 1/4 tsp salt
- 1/2 tsp cream of tarter
- 1/2 tsp baking soda
- 1/2 tbsp ground cinnamon

Directions

1. Insert wire rack in rack position 6. Select bake, set temperature 350 F, timer for 8 minutes. Press start to preheat the oven.
2. In mixing bowl, beat together sugar, butter, and oil until smooth and creamy.
3. Add vanilla and egg and beat until combine.
4. Sift together flour, cinnamon, salt, cream of tartar and baking soda. Add slowly in the egg mixture and mix well until combine.
5. Using cookie scoop drop dough into a baking tray and bake for 8 minutes.
6. Serve and enjoy.

Nutritional Value (Amount per Serving):
- Calories 95
- Fat 5.8 g
- Carbohydrates 9.7 g
- Protein 1.0 g
- Sugar 3.6 g
- Cholesterol 12 mg

Vanilla Peanut Butter Cookies

Prep Time	Cook Time	Serving
10 Minutes	10 Minutes	60

Ingredients

- 2 large eggs
- 2 tsp baking soda
- 1/2 tsp salt
- 1 cup peanut butter
- 1 cup brown sugar
- 1 cup of sugar
- 3 cups flour
- 1 cup vegetable shortening
- 1 1/2 tsp vanilla extract

Directions

1. Insert wire rack in rack position 6. Select bake, set temperature 350 F, timer for 10 minutes. Press start to preheat the oven.
2. In mixing bowl, beat together shortening, brown sugar and sugar until creamy.
3. Add eggs, flour, vanilla extract, baking soda, salt, and peanut butter. Mix well until combine.
4. Make 1-inch balls from dough then roll balls in sugar and place onto a baking tray. Using the back of the spoon slightly flatten balls.
5. Bake for 10 minutes.
6. Serve and enjoy.

Nutritional Value (Amount per Serving):
- Calories 72
- Fat 2.4 g
- Carbohydrates 11.3 g
- Protein 1.9 g
- Sugar 6.1 g
- Cholesterol 6 mg

Easy Brown Sugar Cookies

Prep Time	Cook Time	Serving
10 Minutes	8 Minutes	40

Ingredients

- 1 large egg
- 1 cup sour milk
- 1 tsp baking soda
- 1/2 cup butter, softened
- 1 1/2 cup brown sugar
- 2 1/2 cups flour
- 1/4 tsp salt
- 1 tsp baking powder

Directions

1. Insert wire rack in rack position 6. Select bake, set temperature 375 F, timer for 30 minutes. Press start to preheat the oven.
2. In mixing bowl, beat together butter, sugar, and egg until creamy.
3. Sift together flour, baking powder, and salt. Add baking soda into the milk and stir well.
4. Add milk and dry ingredients alternately into the egg mixture. Mix well.
5. Drop teaspoonfuls batter onto a baking tray and bake for 8 minutes.
6. Serve and enjoy.

Nutritional Value (Amount per Serving):
- Calories 71
- Fat 2.5 g
- Carbohydrates 11.4 g
- Protein 1.0 g
- Sugar 5.3 g
- Cholesterol 11 mg

Healthy Banana Cake

Prep Time	Cook Time	Serving
10 Minutes	40 Minutes	8

Ingredients

- 2 large eggs, beaten
- 1 1/2 cup sugar, granulated
- 1 tsp vanilla extract
- 1/2 cup butter
- 1 cup milk
- 2 cups all-purpose flour
- 2 bananas, mashed
- 1 tsp baking soda
- 1 tsp baking powder

Directions

1. Grease baking dish with butter and set aside.
2. Insert wire rack in rack position 6. Select bake, set temperature 350 F, timer for 40 minutes. Press start to preheat the oven.
3. In a mixing bowl, beat together sugar and butter until creamy. Add beaten eggs and mix well.
4. Add milk, vanilla extract, baking soda, baking powder, flour, and mashed bananas into the mixture and beat for 2 minutes. Mix well.
5. Pour batter into the prepared baking dish and bake for 40 minutes.
6. Serve and enjoy.

Nutritional Value (Amount per Serving):
- Calories 334
- Fat 11.0 g
- Carbohydrates 56.0 g
- Protein 5.0 g
- Sugar 34.2 g
- Cholesterol 64 mg

Chocolate Chip Cake

Prep Time	Cook Time	Serving
10 Minutes	45 Minutes	10

Ingredients

- 2 eggs
- 1 3/4 cups flour
- 1 cup vegetable shortening
- 2 tbsp cocoa powder, unsweetened
- 1 tsp salt
- 1 tsp baking soda
- 3/4 cup chocolate chips
- 1 cup boiling water
- 1 tsp vanilla extract
- 1 cup of sugar

Directions

1. Grease baking dish with butter and set aside.
2. Insert wire rack in rack position 6. Select bake, set temperature 350 F, timer for 45 minutes. Press start to preheat the oven.
3. In mixing bowl, combine together flour, cocoa powder, salt, and baking soda. Set aside.
4. In another bowl, beat together sugar and shortening until creamy.
5. Add egg and vanilla and beat for 2 minutes.
6. Add flour mixture into the shortening mixture and fold well.
7. Pour boiling water into the batter and mix until combine.
8. Add chocolate chips into the batter and fold well.
9. Pour batter into the prepared baking dish and bake for 45 minutes.
10. Slices and serve.

Nutritional Value (Amount per Serving):
- Calories 238
- Fat 5.0 g
- Carbohydrates 44.9 g
- Protein 4.5 g
- Sugar 26.7 g
- Cholesterol 36 mg

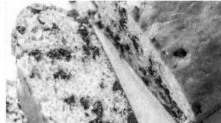

Easy Oatmeal Cake

Prep Time	Cook Time	Serving
10 Minutes	40 Minutes	8

Ingredients

- 2 large eggs
- 1 cup powdered sugar
- 1 cup brown sugar
- 1/2 cup margarine
- 1 1/2 cups flour
- 1 tsp vanilla extract
- 1 1/2 tsp baking soda
- 1 tsp ground cinnamon
- 1 1/2 cups warm water
- 1 cup quick oats
- 1 tsp salt

Directions

1. Grease baking dish with butter and set aside.
2. Insert wire rack in rack position 6. Select bake, set temperature 350 F, timer for 40 minutes. Press start to preheat the oven.
3. Mix together quick oats and warm water. Set aside.
4. In a mixing bowl, beat together sugar, brown sugar and margarine until creamy.
5. Add eggs, salt, cinnamon, baking soda, vanilla, and flour mix until combine.
6. Add oats and water mixture into the batter and fold well.
7. Pour batter into the prepared baking dish and bake for 40 minutes.
8. Slice and serve.

Nutritional Value (Amount per Serving):
- Calories 373
- Fat 13.5 g
- Carbohydrates 58.1 g
- Protein 5.5 g
- Sugar 32.6 g
- Cholesterol 47 mg

Delicious Amish Cake

Prep Time	Cook Time	Serving
10 Minutes	25 Minutes	6

Ingredients

- 1 large egg
- 1/2 tsp salt
- 1 1/4 cups flour
- 3 tbsp butter, melted
- 1/2 cup milk
- 2 tsp baking powder
- 1/2 cup sugar
- For nut topping:
- 1 tbsp butter
- 4 tbsp nuts, chopped
- 4 tbsp brown sugar
- 2 tsp ground cinnamon
- 1 tbsp flour

Directions

1. Grease baking dish with butter and set aside.
2. Insert wire rack in rack position 6. Select bake, set temperature 375 F, timer for 25 minutes. Press start to preheat the oven.
3. For the topping: In a small bowl, mix together cinnamon, flour, nuts, and brown sugar. Add butter and mix until coarse crumbs. Set aside.
4. In a large bowl, mix together flour, salt, baking powder, and sugar.
5. In a separate bowl whisk together melted butter, egg, and milk. Pour into the flour mixture and stir well until combine.
6. Pour batter into the prepared baking dish.
7. Sprinkle nut topping on top of cake batter and bake for 25 minutes.
8. Slice and serve.

Nutritional Value (Amount per Serving):

- Calories 312
- Fat 12.2 g
- Carbohydrates 47.3 g
- Protein 5.7 g
- Sugar 23.8 g
- Cholesterol 53 mg

Sophia

SANDERSON

thank you for purchasing and reading my book.

is the result of many years of study, experience,
harmony and passion,

we hope that the recipes have helped you color
and embellish your tables.
if you liked this diet also try to take a look at my
series of books.

leave a review if you like, can't wait to hear your
feedback!
thanks again, regards, chef Sophia

CPSIA information can be obtained
at www.ICGtesting.com
Printed in the USA
BVHW011120080221
599628BV00012B/791